ADOPTION
The Facts, Feelings, and Issues of a Double Heritage

ADOPTION
The Facts, Feelings, and Issues of a Double Heritage

Jeanne DuPrau

Julian Messner  New York

Fourth Printing, 1983

JULIAN MESSNER and colophon are trademarks of
Simon & Schuster.

Library of Congress Cataloging in Publication Data

DuPrau, Jeanne.
    Adoption: the facts, feelings, and issues of a double heritage.

    Bibliography: p. 121
    Includes index.
    Summary: Discusses the legal and emotional aspects of the adop-
tion process and examines the current movement for giving the
adoptee free access to the records concerning his or her origin.
    1. Adoption—United States—Juvenile literature. [1. Adoption]
I. Title.
HV875.D87   362.7'34'0973   81-11007
ISBN 0-671-34067-0   AACR2

Manufactured in the United States of America.

Design by Irving Perkins Associates.

Contents

68083

Prologue: Scenes from Two Lives

It was Saturday and Gary's father was heading for the lumber yard where he worked. "Want to come along today?" he asked. Gary, who was fifteen, decided he would. At the yard, they ran into a new employee, a man who didn't yet know Gary. "Jeff, I'd like you to meet my son," said Gary's father.

The man smiled. "I could have guessed he was your boy," he said. "He looks just like you."

Gary grinned at his father, and his father grinned back and gave him a quick wink. They liked being told that they looked alike, and it was also one of their favorite private jokes. Gary is an adopted son.

For a long time, Priscilla, a young woman of eighteen years, had been saving her money to buy a car. Every month she'd put part of her paycheck into a special bank account that she shared with her mother. Little by little the total grew until she had just about enough.

Then one day Priscilla's mother told her that she'd withdrawn the car money from the bank. She wouldn't say why. Priscilla felt betrayed and furious. Her mother had taken money out of their account before, but this was money Priscilla had been counting on. She couldn't understand it.

What Priscilla didn't know was that her mother was being blackmailed. Her father, who had left the family when Priscilla was a child, had found a way to get himself some extra money whenever he needed it simply by playing on his wife's greatest fear. He threatened to tell his daughter the secret her mother had guarded grimly for eighteen years—that Priscilla was an adopted child.

The strongbox containing the adoption papers was kept under the refrigerator. Gary knew it, and his parents knew he knew it. They had shown him the papers, in fact, when he was eleven. He even knew his birth mother's last name.

Even so, every now and then when his parents weren't home, Gary would reach beneath the refrigerator and take out the box. He'd open it and look at the papers for a while, just sitting there by himself in the kitchen. He wasn't being sneaky; after all, the box didn't contain any secrets. But those papers were about his life. They made him curious. Somehow, he needed to get them out and think about them from time to time, alone.

When Priscilla was nineteen, her mother died. Her father had been more or less out of touch with the family for years, so it was up to Priscilla to sort through her mother's papers and belongings. She ran across a bill addressed to her parents from a lawyer; when she looked at it, she saw her own name on the page. It was the bill for the lawyer's services in arranging her adoption.

She was astonished. It had never occurred to her that she might be adopted. But just then she couldn't think too much about it. Her mother's death had been such a shock that she didn't have room for another. Besides, she knew she couldn't have been more loved if she *had* been her mother's own child. She didn't feel angry or betrayed.

But several months later, she called the adoption agency that had placed her. They sent her a file of "nonidentifying" information, all that they could legally give out. It contained no names, no addresses, just general descriptions of her father and mother by birth. But those descriptions suddenly added a fascinating new dimension to her life. She was her parents' child, yes—but she was someone else's, too.

It was New Year's Eve. Gary, who had recently graduated from college, was at the family party with his girl friend. Everyone was having a good time and a lot to drink.

Somehow the subject of Gary's adoption came up. This wasn't unusual; it was an open subject in the family, and everyone was comfortable enough with it even to make jokes. Gary's grandmother, for instance, had once said, "It's a good thing he's adopted. Can you imagine what he'd look like if he had our genes?"

Tonight, however, what came out was different. Gary's mother suddenly said, "If you ever go searching for your natural mother, it'll be as if you'd slapped me in the face."

Gary was stunned. His mother had never said anything like that before. In the back of his mind, he had already decided that someday he wanted to meet his birth parents. But if his mother felt that way about it . . .

Gary pushed the thoughts away and brought his mind back to the party. But the questions stayed with him. Had his mother flared up like that just because she was drinking? Or was she really afraid that if Gary looked for his birth parents he would abandon his adoptive family?

Gary never did find out. But for the next four years, he shoved the idea of searching for his birth parents into the background. Not until after his mother died did he decide to do something about it.

In the file sent by the adoption agency, Priscilla read about the two people who were her first parents. Her mother, the paper said, was a young Ethiopian woman who had come to the United States as an exchange student. She was twenty-four and had been married since she was fourteen to a man much older than she. As was common in her country for people of the upper class, hers was an arranged marriage.

In the United States she met a young man, also from Ethiopia, also a student. The two of them became lovers, and before long the woman was pregnant.

She couldn't possibly go home to Ethiopia with a baby. Doing so could actually have put her life in danger. So she gave up the baby, a girl, for adoption before she left the country.

In the time it took to read the file, Priscilla's picture of herself had changed. By upbringing, she was a middle-class black American. By birth, she was not American but pure Ethiopian, on both sides. It was an exciting discovery, and it led her into a search that opened up a whole new world.

In many ways, Gary and Priscilla are very different from each other. Gary grew up in a medium-sized town in California, where his father owned a lumber yard. Priscilla spent a large part of her childhood in Germany, where her father was in the air force. Gary was close to both his parents. Priscilla felt close only to her mother; her father was hardly ever around. Gary has known he was adopted for as long as he can remember; Priscilla didn't find out until she was nineteen years old. Gary is a white man; Priscilla is a black woman.

Besides being college graduates in their twenties, being adopted is about all Gary and Priscilla have in common. It may not seem like much; after all, it's something that took place years ago, when they were very young. But in a way, being adopted is an important bond. It's almost as though

Priscilla and Gary are members of a special club that non-adopted people don't belong to.

Everybody's life is a story. The plots of the stories are all different, though they may have similar features: a person is born, goes to school, makes friends, gets married, and so on. Adopted people, of course, do all those things. But their stories have one particular subplot in addition: they are born to one set of parents; they are, for one reason or another, given up for adoption; and they are raised by another set of parents. Their heritage, unlike most people's, is double: part of it comes to them from their adoptive parents and part from the biological parents they never knew.

Because of this, adopted people think about things and feel things that nonadopted people don't. Adoption, for them, doesn't end when the papers are signed. It affects their entire lives, as it affects the lives of their birth parents and their adoptive parents. It doesn't necessarily make them happier or less happy than other people, but it does, in certain ways, make them different. No one who is not adopted has had experiences quite like Gary's and Priscilla's.

There are an estimated five million adopted people in the United States—more than in any other country—and millions more who are the birth parents, adoptive parents, sisters, brothers, and other relatives of adopted people. This book will tell you their story. It's a story that has at its heart the themes of birth, family, and personal identity —crucial matters for everyone. It involves tangled nets of circumstance, deep and complicated emotions, mysteries, weird coincidences, and fierce feuds. And its cast of characters is huge and various. People of wealth and position are part of it (like President Ronald Reagan, for instance, who has an adopted son), as are people with neither, like the war orphans of Vietnam. The fourteen-year-old girl who has a baby she can't keep is part of it, and the couple down the street who have been trying for years to have children, and the welfare mother whose troubles make baby number six unwelcome. Gary and Priscilla are part of it, and maybe, in one way or another, you are, too.

PART I

Child plus Parents: The Facts of Adoption

CHAPTER 1

The Homeless Children

It can happen in a number of ways. A mother and father die in an accident. A young girl becomes pregnant unintentionally and has a baby she doesn't want to keep. A single woman, ill and poor, decides she can't take care of her children. A flood occurs—or an earthquake or a war—and large numbers of people are killed. Events like these have happened all through history and go on happening today. Whether personal misfortune or large-scale disaster, they all have at least one thing in common: they leave behind children who have no homes.

When such things happen today, all kinds of social service agencies stand ready to help. One will provide temporary shelter for the homeless children, feeding and watching out for them until they have someplace else to go. Another will find foster homes for them and provide money for the foster parents to use in their upkeep. Still another will arrange for them, when possible, to be permanently adopted into new families.

But such an organized concern about children with no homes is relatively recent. In earlier times, social service agencies did not exist. Of course, the accidents, wars, and unwanted births happened anyway, and children were left homeless and needed to be cared for. What became of them depended on what period of history they happened to be born in—and how lucky they were.

In colonial times, it was not at all uncommon for children to find themselves without parents. Life in the wild, unsettled New World was hard, and hardships often began even before the colonists set foot in America. During the long voyage across the Atlantic Ocean, people had little besides salted meat and hard biscuits to eat. They lived in crowded, stuffy spaces below the deck, and standards of cleanliness were necessarily low. Sometimes illness would sweep through a boatload of people like a brushfire, and when the boat arrived in America, some of the children who had set out with their parents from Europe would be orphans.

Families who survived the ocean voyage and established themselves in one of the colonies had to face other dangers. Cold winters, failing crops, unfamiliar diseases, and accidents all took their toll, and sometimes, again, children were left without parents.

One of the most common ways for a child to lose a mother was for the mother to die in childbirth. No particular sanitary procedures were used in delivering children in those days; no special techniques or equipment were available when the birth turned out to be difficult. One historian has estimated that, in the early colonies, about one birth in thirty caused the mother's death. Sometimes a father, left with six or eight young motherless children, had no way to take care of them, and they became orphans, in effect if not in fact.

Families were large in those days. Birth control methods didn't exist, of course, and even if they had, few people would have wanted to use them. Scraping a living from the wilderness was a lot of work, and the more hands there were to help with it, the better. So couples continued to have children throughout the woman's childbearing years. The last few children might be born when their mother was in her forties and their father in his fifties or older. Because life expectancies then were not as long as they are now, these children might still be quite young when their parents died.

When colonists were faced with the problem of a homeless child—and, for all these reasons, that happened fairly often—they had several possible solutions. The easiest was for a relative or a neighbor to take in the orphan. The extra person to help with the work compensated for the extra mouth to feed, and the new child would be treated as a full-fledged member of the family.

Another possibility existed for boys, if they were old enough: they could be taken on as apprentices. This meant that a contract was drawn up between a boy and the man who would become his master. The master would agree to teach the boy his trade—which might be wagon making, printing, silversmithing, or any other—and to provide him with food, shelter, parental guidance, and discipline for the term of the contract. In return, the boy would agree to work hard and to obey his master in all things, just as he would obey his own father.

Girls could be taken in on this basis, too. But instead of learning a trade, they learned the only skills thought necessary of a girl—those of a homemaker. Everyone assumed that all girls would become wives and mothers, as most of them did. They were taught to read and write, and with that their education usually ended.

For some children, being an apprentice worked out very well. The apprentice was more or less adopted into the master's family and so had the benefits of family life and learned useful skills as well. For others, the situation was not so good. The master might be harsh or cruel, or he might neglect the apprentice's training and just have him sweep the barn and feed the chickens. Sometimes an unhappy apprentice could appeal to the law for his rights; most often, he suffered in silence or ran away.

Just about all homeless children in colonial times either went to live with relatives or became apprentices. But if they had no relatives and were too young to be apprenticed, they might be sent instead to the almshouse, if there happened to be one in town. An almshouse was a place where people who were too poor or ill to take care of themselves could come for assistance. Only the larger towns were likely to have one. Children who ended up here would find themselves in the company of people of all ages and conditions, from the temporarily penniless to the chronically ill or insane. It was not a desirable place to be; fortunately, few children stayed there very long.

Living with relatives, becoming apprentices, or going to the almshouse—in the years following the American Revolution, these continued to be the alternatives for homeless children. As the nineteenth century approached, however, conditions in America began to change. Immigrants began to pour into the country. The cities and towns were growing; it was no longer difficult to find people to help with the work. Soon it was easier for a farmer or a tradesman to hire an immigrant, who would work for very little, than to take in an orphan, who would require care for years. By the 1840s, the apprentice system was dead.

At the same time, the number of homeless children was rising, especially in the cities. Immigrants by the thousand crowded together in the city slums. They were poor and uneducated, and they often could not speak English, so they had to take whatever work they could find, and it was likely to be grueling work that paid almost nothing. Many immigrants found that they could not support their families; their children, even those as young as seven or eight, would leave home to live on the streets, hoping to do better for themselves by selling newspapers or chestnuts than their parents had been able to do for them. Other children's parents died of tuberculosis, or spent all their time drinking, or simply abandoned their families and disappeared. These children too were out on the street, sleeping in doorways, staying alive by doing what work they could, or by stealing.

The old ways were no longer adequate to cope with the situation. People began to look closely at what was happening in their society and to talk more and more about social problems and the reforms that they thought would solve them. The existence of so many homeless children was among the most pressing issues. It was no good to keep putting them into almshouses, the reformers argued; they were bound to be neglected there and thrown in with bad company. Almshouse children weren't likely to grow up to be respectable and useful members of society. In fact, they might easily grow up to be drifters or criminals. But what else was there to do with these children if they had no relatives to go to and no one wanted their labor?

The answer—seized enthusiastically by the social reformers—was the orphanage. In the 1830s orphanages began springing up all over the country. They took in not only orphans but other needy children as well—those who had been abandoned and those whose families were too poor or sick to take care of them. At an orphanage, children would get not only food and shelter but also education, training in work, and guidance in morals and correct behavior. It seemed like an excellent way to provide for homeless children and at the same time to improve society by catching trouble before it began. By the 1850s thousands of homeless children were living in orphanages.

Living in an orphanage may have been better, in some ways, than living on the streets or in a desperately poor home; at least the meals were regular, and there were beds to sleep in. But an orphanage didn't take the place of a family. Most of them were large, solid, stern-looking buildings that housed perhaps two hundred children. The children slept in large rooms where the beds were lined up in orderly rows, perhaps twenty beds to a room. In a typical orphan asylum, the children got up at dawn, went to a service in the chapel, and then went to breakfast. They marched from one place to another in line, two by two, holding hands with their partners, boys and girls separately. Often they were not allowed to talk. They ate at long tables, and when everyone was through, they filed out, quietly, two by two, and went to their classrooms, where they would spend the morning. They might spend the afternoon there, too, or they might go instead to a shop class, where they would learn a trade. Always, the children were required to move through the day in a quiet, orderly, obedient fashion. If they did not, they would be punished. For minor disobedience they might be deprived of a play period or put for a while on a diet of bread and water; for a major wrongdoing, they might be whipped or even locked to a ball and chain and put into a cell. In most orphanages, order and obedience were the chief values; there was not much room for warmth and affection.

The Children's Aid Society, founded by Charles Loring Brace in New York in 1853, understood this lack and came up with a plan that took into account a child's need to belong to a family. Beginning in 1854, the society rounded up groups of homeless children and put them on immigrant trains headed for the midwestern states. In that part of the country, which was sparsely populated compared with the East, extra help for farms and businesses was still in demand. The idea was to match the children with families who needed extra hands, thereby satisfying the needs of everyone.

The plan worked pretty well. Plenty of street children, scraping along as beggars, rag sellers, or match peddlers, were eager to go out west in hope of finding a home. One bunch after another, escorted by people from the society, boarded the trains, leaving everything familiar behind, and traveled to towns in Michigan, Illinois, Iowa, and Wisconsin. There they would be ushered into a church or town hall, the people of the town would crowd in to look them over, and the process of choosing would begin. It must have been rather hard on the children, lined up on display, wondering who, if anyone, was going to pick them. But most of the matches, according to the society's records, worked out well. In all, homes were found in this way for about twenty thousand children.

The people who founded orphanages and organizations like the Children's Aid Society were of course concerned with the future of the children they were trying to help. But they were equally concerned—in fact, often more concerned—with the future of society. When they walked the streets of the city and saw little boys who had turned to theft and begging to support themselves, and young girls who had turned to prostitution, they were as worried about the effect of these children on others as they were about the plight of the children themselves. Charles Brace, founder of the Children's Aid Society, issued a warning: "These boys and girls, it should be remembered, will soon form the great lower class of our city. They will influence elections; they may shape the policy of the city; they will, assuredly, if unreclaimed, poison society all around them. They will help form the great multitude of robbers, thieves, vagrants, and prostitutes who are now such a burden upon the law-respecting community."

This was why the discipline in asylums was so strict: the most important thing, in the minds of those who ran the orphanages, was to bring the children into line, so that by the time they left they would have been transformed into upright, law-abiding citizens. It did not occur to people that there was any better way to do this than by requiring rigid order and handing out harsh punishments to those who resisted it.

But as time went on, a suspicion arose in people's minds that something was missing from the orphanages. They bore a strong resemblance to prisons, or to army camps. The young people who emerged from them were not necessarily ideal citizens, and even if they had been, using such unrelenting harshness to make them so would have been questionable. "A human soul needs more than work, good as work is," said the general secretary of the Associated Charities of Boston in 1888, "and some provision must be made for pleasures, for an occasional hour of freedom, and for society." The good of the child was at last becoming the primary concern. And the best place for a child, it began to seem, was, after all, in a family.

Organizations like the Children's Aid Society increased their efforts to place children in homes rather than in institutions. There were problems involved, however. Critics accused these organizations of placing children too hastily, without making sure first that the homes were good ones. They also claimed that no one checked on the children after they had been in their new families for a while, and they feared that many children might be badly treated. To counter these charges, the agencies sent out investigators who looked into the character and finances of families applying for children and who later reported how hard the children were worked and whether or not they were sent to church on Sundays, given enough food and clothing, and allowed to go to school.

The status of children in these families was rather vague. They were not exactly servants, but they were not full-fledged members of the family, either. The family could "discharge" the child at any time, if he or she was found "useless or otherwise unsatisfactory." The children were free to leave, if they didn't like the way things were going, and some, unaccustomed to answering to anyone, made off the first time they were punished or scolded. Gradually people realized that such a loose arrangement allowed for all kinds of abuses and that it was important to have laws safeguarding children's welfare.

The first state to pass a law permitting legal adoption was Massachusetts, in 1851. Slowly, other states followed.

Over the next seventy-five years, they all passed laws having to do with adoption. The laws differ from state to state, but in general they all deal with the same issues:
- Who may adopt and who may be adopted?
- Whose consent must be given?
- How must the adoption be carried out?
- What are the rights and duties of the people involved?

Whether or not people are eligible to adopt children depends first of all on how old they are and where they live. In most states, only a legal adult (eighteen or twenty-one years old) who is a resident of the state may adopt. Sometimes an adopting person must be a certain number of years older—usually around ten—than the person to be adopted.

Some state laws require that the race and/or religion of the adoptive parents match that of the child. Recently, however, the legality of such restrictions is being called into question. Laws forbidding interracial adoption have in some cases been found unconstitutional.

Most states permit the adoption of both children and adults. Consent to the adoption must always be obtained from the birth mother (and sometimes from the father) unless she is judged to have abandoned the child or unless her rights have been legally terminated by a judge who has found her incompetent to care for the child. The adopting parents must give their consent to the adoption, of course, and so must any child over a certain age—in most states twelve or fourteen.

Some states require that all adoptions be arranged by licensed agencies. Others permit private arrangements between the mother and the adoptive parents. In both kinds of adoptions, there must be an investigation of the adoptive home to make sure it's a suitable one.

To make the adoption final, all states require a court hearing during which a judge signs the adoption decree. At this point, all the rights and responsibilities of parenthood are turned over to the adoptive parents, and at the same time those rights and responsibilities are ended for the birth parents. From then on, in the eyes of the law, the adoptive parents are the real and only parents of that child.

These laws establish, at last, an adopted child's place in the family: it is exactly the same as that of a natural daughter or son. Every state had passed adoption laws by 1929, and the number of families who wanted to adopt was soaring. From then on, legal adoption became the first-choice solution to the problem of homeless children.

CHAPTER 2

How Adoption Works Today

Melissa is seventeen and a junior in high school. For over a year, she's been going out with Steve, a senior, and they consider their relationship serious. They began sleeping together about six months ago; both of them wanted sexual intimacy, and Melissa felt safe from pregnancy because Steve either used condoms or "stopped just in time" (he said he knew exactly when that was). Although they have not actually talked about it, Melissa imagines that she and Steve will eventually be married.

One month, Melissa misses her period. She can't believe anything has gone wrong, however, since she and Steve have always been so careful. She's heard that illness or stress can make you miss your period, and she had the flu not long ago. That must be the problem, she decides. She waits a while longer. But there is no sign of her period, and she begins feeling nauseated now and then. Without telling anyone, she goes to a clinic and has a pregnancy test. It comes out positive; she is pregnant.

Melissa is in a fix that about a million teenage girls find themselves in every year. Some, like Melissa, are white; others are of minority races. Some are from poor, inner city, or rural families, often with only one parent. Others, like Melissa, are from relatively stable, middle-class, suburban homes. Most are between fifteen and nineteen years old; but about thirty thousand are younger.

So Melissa has a lot of company in her predicament. It doesn't do her much good, however; she doesn't know anyone her age who is pregnant. She feels totally alone.

Her first thought is to let Steve know. But when she does, she is surprised and angry at his response. "Don't blame me," he says nervously. "I was careful, wasn't I? Can't you just get rid of it?" Suddenly the love he has said he feels for her seems to have disappeared. He is not unkind, exactly; he's just distant and uneasy. He says he has no intention of marrying her or anyone right now. He is too young to be a father. He has other things to do.

Stunned, Melissa faces her choices. She can get an abortion. (In her state, they are available free.) She can have the baby and keep it. Or she can have the baby and give it up for adoption.

After a few days of private agony, Melissa decides to tell her parents what has happened. They are shocked and upset, but after a while they realize that anger and disapproval will not solve the problem and begin trying to get Melissa some help. They find a counseling service at the same clinic where Melissa had her pregnancy test and Melissa makes an appointment to talk to one of the counselors. (Agencies that offer counseling to pregnant women are listed in the section Sources of Help at the end of this book.)

In the meantime, thoughts have been spinning wildly around in her head. Abortion seems like the easiest answer: one quick treatment, and the whole problem disappears. But somehow Melissa recoils from the idea of abortion. She knows that she has a living being inside her; already it is more than two months old and has eyes and a mouth, hands and feet. In her mind, this baby is already a person, and it's hers.

She begins to imagine how it would be to have a baby

of her own. She sees herself in a small, cozy apartment with sunlight coming in through the window, holding her baby, feeding it, playing with it, making baby clothes. She is sure she would be a good mother. The picture she imagines appeals to her more and more. She feels as though she has made up her mind: she will quit school, have the baby, and keep it.

When the day of her appointment arrives, she explains this plan to the counselor, a young woman who seems friendly and sympathetic. The counselor listens, nods, and then asks some questions. How will Melissa support herself and the baby in this apartment? What kind of job can a girl who is not a high school graduate get? Who will look after the baby while Melissa is at work? What if Melissa wants to go to a movie now and then, or to a friend's house? She will have to get sitters and pay for them. The baby will demand both her time and her money, and Melissa's life will be far more work than play.

As she thinks about these questions, two new concerns enter Melissa's thoughts. One is for herself. By keeping the baby, what will she be doing to her own life? Will she ever go back to school? Will she be cutting herself off from her friends? What about boys? How will they feel about going out with a girl who has a child?

The other concern is for the unborn baby. Will she be able to provide a good life for a child, not just when it's a baby, but when it's five years old, ten, fifteen? Will she be willing and able to give the time and attention a child needs to grow up healthy and happy?

These questions are on her mind as she goes home from the counseling center, and in the weeks that follow, she turns them around and around, over and over again, deciding first one way and then the other. She talks to a few people—the counselor, a couple of friends—but mostly, as the months pass and she feels the child coming to life inside her, Melissa keeps her thoughts to herself. By the time she is in her sixth month of pregnancy, she thinks that she has made her decision. Though one voice in her is saying that she already loves this baby and wants it, another voice tells her that it wouldn't be fair, either to herself or to the child, to keep it.

The counselor at the clinic refers her to an adoption agency, and she meets with a social worker there. The social worker explains the procedure.

"Sometimes," she says, "it's difficult for a girl to live at home during the last months of pregnancy. If you want, you could come into one of the hostels the agency runs for young women about to have their babies. You'd have the company of people who are facing similar problems, and counseling and medical services would be available. Whether you'd like to stay in one of these hostels is up to you.

"We don't want you to make any final decisions or sign any papers until the baby arrives. You'll have a chance to see the baby and hold it. Then you'll make your decision. We don't want you to sign away your parental rights and then change your mind after the baby is born.

"Once you've decided to place the baby for adoption, you will sign a legal agreement ending your rights as a parent. We'll select a family for the child, and we'll tell you something about them. But you won't know their names or where they live, and they won't have that information about you. What you will know is that everything possible has been done to ensure that your child will have a good home."

Melissa decides to spend her remaining time at the agency hostel. Though her parents are doing their best to be understanding, things at home are tense sometimes, and she needs to get away. Three months later, Melissa has a baby boy and makes the final decision to place him for adoption.

Two years before, about the time Melissa started going out with Steve, Phil and Susan, a couple in their early thirties, began to think about adopting a child. They had always assumed they would have a family, but in the six years of their marriage, Susan had not become pregnant. Medical tests failed to pinpoint the reason for the couple's inability to have a child. By now, both Phil and Susan have accepted, with much sadness, that they will not have biological children. But their desire for a family remains. They call an adoption agency in their city and make an appointment to talk to one of the social workers.

What they learn at that first meeting is both interesting and disappointing. The social worker tells them that right now far more people want to adopt babies than there are babies available for adoption. This is especially true if they want a healthy, white infant. If they are willing to take a child with a handicap, or a child who is more than two years old, or a child of a race different from theirs, they might have an easier time. Otherwise, they will be put on a waiting list. The wait might be several years.

"Suppose we decide to put our names on the waiting list?" Susan asks. "What happens then?"

The social worker explains that the next step is a "home study." A person from the adoption agency will visit Phil and Susan's home and interview them, both together and separately. They will answer questions about their marriage, about their reasons for wanting a child, about their financial situation, and about themselves. There will be several of these visits, and by the time they are over, the agency will have some facts and some feelings about what kind of parents Phil and Susan might make. In a few weeks, they will send the couple a letter either accepting or rejecting their application to adopt.

Phil frowns worriedly. "We're not wealthy people," he says. "Will that count against us?"

"No," says the social worker. "We're just interested in making sure you can support a child. You don't have to be rich."

Susan has a question, too. "For what reasons do you reject people?" she asks.

"Sometimes we find that people don't really want to adopt a child, or aren't ready to yet. They may still be grieving or bitter about not having biological children and may not be able to accept an adopted child as their own. They may be hoping that a child will keep their crumbling marriage together. It isn't fair to the children to place them in situations like those."

On their way home, Phil and Susan discuss what they've learned and come to a decision: they will put their names on the agency's waiting list. After several months, the home study is made, and Phil and Susan receive a letter not long afterward saying that they have been accepted as adoptive parents. Then there is nothing left to do but wait. At last, almost two years after they first put in their application, the call comes. A baby boy is at the agency, ready to be taken home.

And so the two halves of the process come together: the woman who places a baby for adoption and the couple who want a child. The baby's birth certificate is changed, so that his last name is given as the name of the adoptive parents. Then the records—the original birth certificate, the adoption papers, the relinquishment signed by the birth parents—are put into a file and "sealed." This means that they are permanently closed except to the social workers at the agency. It is not legal for the birth mother, the adoptive parents, or the adopted child to look at that information. Officially, Phil and Susan's baby is now just as much a member of his new family as if he had been born to them.

Several thousand adoptions more or less like this one

occur every year. No one knows exactly how many, though, since there is no central office for collecting the statistics. Each state keeps its own records separately and is not required to report its figures to the federal government. In California there were 2,170 agency adoptions in 1979. In New York there were 2,071. Other states are likely to have had fewer adoptions than populous New York and California, so the national number is probably quite a bit under 100,000. But the only way to know for sure would be to get the statistics for all the states and add them together.

Agency adoptions are only part of the picture, however. There are other kinds of adoptions as well. About half of all adoptions are by relatives of the child. If a child suddenly loses his parents in an accident, for example, his aunt and uncle or his grandparents will often adopt him. This can be true, too, for the child of an unmarried woman who decides to keep her baby and then discovers, after a year or so, that she cannot keep him after all. Sometimes her parents or the family of a brother or sister will adopt the child. If this is possible, the mother may prefer it to placing the child for adoption with an agency.

Some nonrelative adoptions are made without involving an agency at all. These are called independent adoptions. Suppose, for example, that Melissa had decided she didn't need counseling and didn't want to go through an agency's procedures. She might have asked her doctor if he knew of a couple interested in adopting a child. If he did, the doctor could arrange an independent adoption. A lawyer would draw up the adoption papers, and Melissa would agree to surrender the child to the adopting couple. (She might or might not meet them.) As soon as the baby was born, it would be handed over to its new family.

Phil and Susan might have chosen to adopt this way if they'd been unwilling to wait as long as the agency required, or if they hadn't wanted to go through the agency's interviews and home visits. Through a doctor or lawyer, they would have located a woman who planned to give up her baby for adoption. They might even know someone like this already—Melissa, for instance, might be the daughter of friends of theirs. They would pay a fee to the person who arranged the adoption, and their waiting period would be only the length of time before the baby arrived.

Both independent and agency adoptions have their advantages. Adoption through an agency offers the most protection to the new parents and especially to the child. The agency's in-depth investigation of the adopting family ensures, as well as anything can, that the child's new parents will be good ones. The information the agency records about the biological mother and father, especially medical information, will be useful to the adopting parents. And the privacy of both the biological and adoptive parents is protected; they do not meet each other or know each other's names. (Whether or not this privacy is an advantage is debatable, however; as we'll see later on, some people don't see it that way.)

People who choose independent adoption give up some of the security of an agency adoption. Investigations of the adopting couple and of the background of the biological parents are likely to be less thorough. Because the child's mother and the adoptive parents may meet each other or even know each other already, there's a possibility that the mother may try to maintain some connection with the child, which can cause resentment and confusion. Sometimes, having agreed to the adoption while she was pregnant, the mother changes her mind when she actually sees the baby. If the adoption were being done through an agency, this wouldn't matter; that particular baby would not have been committed to any specific couple, and the mother would not yet have given up her legal rights. If this happens in an independent adoption, however, the agreement may already have been signed. The adoptive parents have been expecting to get the baby, and when they don't they'll be justifiably angry. Such a case might end up as a legal battle.

But independent adoption has its pluses, too. The prospective parents do not have to go through the long series of interviews and visits or the lengthy—and in some people's opinion, nosy—investigation. And a couple can often get a child more quickly this way. Once the pregnant mother and the adopting couple are matched up, the only wait is for the birth of the child.

It's the long agency waiting lists that send many couples in search of independent adoptions. But an independent adoption is not always easy to arrange, for the same reason that the agency waiting lists are so long. The kind of baby most in demand is a healthy, white infant—a baby only a few weeks or months old. These days, few such babies are being put up for adoption.

One reason for this, of course, is birth control. Women today have much more choice than they used to about whether they'll become pregnant or not. Another reason is abortion. Over a million women a year end unwanted pregnancies that way.

In spite of birth control and abortion, however, thousands of babies are born to unwed mothers every year. Around 600,000 of these mothers are teenagers. Of the eleven million sexually active teenagers in this country, only about one in five uses any birth control method at all, some because they don't know what kinds of birth control methods exist or where to get them, some because they're afraid that if they use birth control their parents will find out, but most because fussing with birth control seems to interfere with passion and romance. How can you be spontaneous if you have to interrupt things to get out your birth control devices—your condoms or diaphragms or foam? And not many teenage girls go to the trouble of taking birth control pills. Relying on the Pill, which requires a prescription and has to be taken every day, somehow implies that a girl is expecting to have sexual intercourse often and regularly. For most teenage girls, this is not the case, and even if it is, they still prefer to think of sex as spontaneous and passionate, an image that's hard to reconcile with the practical, everyday common sense of taking the Pill.

As a result, around a million teenagers a year become pregnant and, if they decide against abortion, have babies. In the past, a large percentage of these babies would have been given up for adoption. Today, that's no longer true.

The reason has to do with a change in social attitudes. A woman who had a child out of wedlock used to be severely condemned by society. A pregnant teenager would often be made to feel that she had ruined her life. Her family would do everything possible to hide her condition, and she would give up her baby for adoption at birth. The mother would be likely to accept society's judgment of her. She would be ashamed and depressed. Her illegitimate baby would be a dark secret that she would keep hidden all her life.

Now, however, society's disapproval is not always so harsh. Sex before marriage is far more widely accepted, and unmarried mothers are not looked on with such horror. Many teenage girls today are actually pleased to find out they are pregnant. Even if there are no prospects of marriage to the child's father, the idea of having a baby may seem exciting rather than shameful. A girl who comes from a troubled and unhappy family and whose relationship with her boyfriend has fallen apart may see a baby as a solution to her loneliness—someone of her very own who will love her no matter what. A girl who has wanted to leave home and quit school may see the baby as her chance to do so. Taking care of a baby can give a purpose to a girl who has never had one before; she may see herself, as Melissa did, fixing up an apartment, feeding and playing with her child, bringing it up right, and being happy. Because this vision is so attractive, around 90 percent of the unmarried teenagers who become pregnant and give birth are now keeping their babies.

On the one hand, few young, healthy babies are available; on the other hand, many people are anxious, even desperate, to adopt children. In a situation like this, an adoptable baby becomes very precious. Consequently, a black market in babies has developed in recent years.

Some lawyers have made a profitable business out of finding babies for couples who want to adopt. They seek out pregnant girls—through hospitals, clinics, counseling centers, abortion services—and offer them money to have their babies and put them up for adoption. Often other benefits are offered, too: free medical care, an all-expense-paid "vacation" during the last weeks of pregnancy, and additional money after the baby is born. A girl who might otherwise have had an abortion or have kept her baby is often persuaded by these offers to give up the child for adoption. The lawyer charges his clients, the adoptive parents, a large fee, perhaps ten or fifteen thousand dollars, for his services, because what he's "selling" is so rare and valuable that he can get just about any price he wants.

The main goal of the black market adoption lawyers is not to find a good home for a child who needs one but to find a child for a couple who want one. Nobody investigates the adopting couple to find out if they'll make good parents, and nobody checks after the adoption to see how the child is doing. Parents who have money, whatever kind of people they are, can get a child; parents who don't have money can't, even though they might provide a fine home.

The biological mother can get shortchanged, too. No one takes time before the adoption to find out if she really wants to give up her child or if she is being pressured into it. The lawyers can be very convincing, especially when they are talking to teenagers. A girl may have her baby, give it up, and only then begin to realize that she's only been hearing one side of the story. She may never have had a chance to consider her decision carefully.

What happened to a woman named Cathy is an example of the tangle that a black market adoption can become. When Cathy found that she was pregnant, she was confused and uncertain about what she wanted to do. After several months, she decided against having an abortion and went to a doctor for an examination. The doctor, learning that Cathy was unmarried and was thinking about having the baby adopted, immediately showed an interest in her.

"I have some friends who'd like to adopt a baby," he said. He told Cathy his friends were fine people who would make excellent parents and that a private adoption would be much better for her than an agency adoption. "A private adoption lets you choose your baby's parents," he said. "With an agency, you never know where the child is going."

Cathy wavered. She hadn't made up her mind yet whether she wanted to keep her baby or not. But the doctor, who had seen his chance to make a good sum of money from people who would pay a lot to get a child, began to put pressure on Cathy. He called her constantly, wanting her decision. "These people need· to know," he would say. "We can't keep them hanging." Still, Cathy couldn't make up her mind. It wasn't until just before the baby was born that she decided, desperate just to decide *something*, that she would go ahead with the adoption.

She met the prospective parents in the hospital, just after she'd had the baby. She told them honestly that she still wasn't absolutely sure she wanted to give her baby up. Legally, she had six months to decide. She agreed to let the couple take the baby home during that time.

After three and a half months, Cathy decided that she wanted to keep her baby. Immediately, she was attacked from all sides. The adoptive parents, having become attached to the baby, were heartbroken and furious. Their lawyer harassed Cathy mercilessly, threatening her, trying to make her feel guilty, trying to buy her off. Cathy stood firm, however, and she did get her baby back, but the whole experience was traumatic for her, as it was for the couple who wanted the child. It was the kind of mess that wouldn't have happened if Cathy had not been counseled by someone who probably had several thousand dollars riding on the deal.

Black market adoptions are big business in this country. Joseph Reid, the director of the Child Welfare League of America, estimated in 1978 that a third of all private adoptions were actually black market adoptions. That amounts to about five thousand cases. Reid thinks this figure is probably on the low side. When there are people willing to pay ten or twenty thousand dollars for a child (in one case, the reported price was fifty thousand), there are also likely to be a lot of people determined to cash in on the situation.

Black market adoption thrives because so few healthy white infants are available for adoption. But plenty of other children *are* available—not only available but waiting eagerly for homes. Until recently, many of these children were considered unadoptable. They often spent their entire childhood in institutions and foster homes. But lately people have begun to take a new view of adoption. Adopting a child who is handicapped, more than a year old, or of another race no longer seems inconceivable, and as a result, the whole adoption picture is changing.

CHAPTER *3*

The Special Cases

White, healthy, adoptable infants are in short supply, but that doesn't mean there aren't any children available for adoption. In fact, there are thousands of them—children who desperately need homes and parents. Some are no longer babies and are considered too old to be adopted. Some are children of minority races, and some are handicapped. In the language of adoption agencies, these are called "hard-to-place" children. It's not uncommon for them to wait years to be adopted—or to grow up without ever being adopted at all.

No one really knows how many of these children there are in the United States, because agencies responsible for such children all work separately. You might find out that an agency in Boise, Idaho, has placed 43 children in foster homes, that 157 children live in a children's home in Tulsa, Oklahoma, and that 29 children live in a hospital in New York City. But no one can tell you just how many children throughout the country are waiting to be adopted at any given time.

Adoption agency policies also contribute to the invisibility of hard-to-place children. Since nearly all the people seeking to adopt want healthy white infants, the social workers usually don't bother to suggest children who don't fit that description. Older children, those from minorities, and those that are handicapped are often labeled "unadoptable." After that labeling, no one makes much effort to find them permanent homes.

So the children spend their lives without families. Some are shunted from one foster home to another as foster parents move away, decide not to take in children anymore, or decide they can't handle the child who's been placed with them. Other children live in children's homes of various kinds. Children with serious handicaps might spend their childhood in hospitals.

Of course, foster homes, hospitals, and institutions aren't necessarily terrible places. A child might be happier growing up in a good institution than in a bad family. And some children—the severely retarded, for example, or those with extremely disabling physical or emotional problems—need institutional care. For them, a family is not a real possibility.

But for most of the hard-to-place children, life in foster homes and institutions is definitely second best. They need and want real families—real parents who are going to belong to them for good and real homes that they won't always be in danger of losing. In the past, that wish would have had only a faint chance of coming true. Today, however, the picture is beginning to change.

The baby shortage is one big reason for this change. Some people who haven't been able to find a white, healthy infant to adopt, or who don't want to wait for one, are considering other kinds of children instead—children who are more than two years old, for instance.

Some of these are the children of unmarried teenage girls who fell in love with the idea of being mothers. They decided to keep their babies, only to discover after a year or two that motherhood was simply more than they could handle. Unable to deal with their children, they placed them for adoption, at one, two, or three years old, and sometimes even older. One social worker tells of a mother who brought in her eight-year-old daughter for adoption. The mother was too busy with her work to take care of her and had never been very attached to her anyway. Adoption agencies have noted with alarm that this kind of relinquishment is becoming increasingly common.

Sometimes children's natural parents neglect or abuse them to such an extent that the courts intervene and remove them from their families. This can happen when a neighbor notices that the children down the street seem to be home alone a lot and are always wandering around looking shabby and undernourished. Or a teacher might find that one student falls asleep in class all the time or frequently has bruises that look like the marks of a beating. The neighbor and the teacher call social welfare authorities, and someone is sent to investigate. If the investigator finds that the children are being mistreated, laws exist that allow their removal from the family.

Usually these children are put in foster homes, and their parents are given a chance to straighten out their lives. Sometimes the parents do shape up, and the children go home. Other times, however, the parents' problems don't go away. The children's stay in the foster home stretches on and on. The parents may eventually decide to give up their children. Or, in extreme cases, the court may terminate the parents' rights without their consent. Or the parents may waver endlessly back and forth, unable to take the children back, unwilling to give them up. In the meantime, the children grow up in foster homes, unavailable for adoption by a permanent family until they are too old to be easily placed.

There are also parents who don't mistreat their children but who simply cannot take care of them. Often these are single mothers who have little money, few skills, and many mouths to feed, and who are just plain worn out by the struggle. They put their children in foster homes, intending the arrangement to be temporary, but they cannot improve their situations. They end up placing their children for adoption in the hope of giving them a chance for a better life.

It isn't easy to find adoptive parents for these older children. Most people who adopt want to start fresh with the unformed mind and personality of an infant. They don't want a child who is already attached to natural or foster parents and will have to transfer his or her affections. They worry that a child with a deprived or disturbed background may have emotional problems that will be hard to deal with, or unacceptable ways of doing things that will have to be changed.

Even so, more adoptive parents these days are deciding to take an older child into their family. In many ways, this really is harder than adopting an infant. Most children, for example, struggle with a conflict of loyalties at first, as this father describes:

> She talked about her mother. She remembers her mother as the person who came to see her on Sundays, who always brought a gift, who always combed her hair, who was the charming person. Everything that was unpleasant with us was an unfavorable comparison to the mother, whom she saw once a week, if that often. Her mother had never had any hand at disciplining her; she'd only brought her presents and combed her hair and been nice to her. And of course we suffered a little bit in comparison there, because we'd have to do things. We had to make her eat her vegetables, and we had to cut out the chocolate because of her teeth. We had to make her drink her milk.

In spite of difficulties like these, however, adoptions of older children can work out well. One group of researchers did a study of ninety-one families who adopted older children. Many of them, they found, went through the same process, a time of conflict that gradually grew less intense as the child began to fit into the new family. It's hard for everyone at first, but the rewards make the struggle worthwhile, as experiences like this one show:

I would say the hardest thing was the breaking down of that resistance—that outer shell she had, her determination not to like us. To try to win her over, to try to win her affection—it was a big problem. She tried not to like us.

She's a very affectionate girl now, very affectionate. But it took her a year, and then one night she reached up and she said, "I love you."

In fact, the researchers found that most of the adoptions they studied (they estimated about 85 percent) were successful—that is, both parents and children were happy with each other. They ended their study by encouraging more adoptive parents to give homes to older children.

Of course, older children are not the only ones who are hard to place. Because most people who want to adopt are white, minority children fall into the hard-to-place category, too. Just as the white infant shortage has changed the adoption prospects for older children, it has changed them for minority children as well. But here the issues are more complicated.

Until about fifteen years ago, most adoption agencies were dealing with white parents and white children. Few would have placed a black child in a white family, even if there had been white couples willing to adopt a black child. And black families, seeing adoption agencies as basically white organizations, rarely applied there. Their adoptions were likely to be private and often involved the children of friends and relatives.

But with the growth of the civil rights movement in the 1960s, this situation changed. A lot of white Americans began to look at black people with new understanding and respect and also to feel they had some responsibility to help blacks gain the equality that had been denied them for so long. For the first time, white couples began to think about adopting black children.

Some couples had social or political motives: they wanted to give a black child a chance for a better life, show that integration could work, or take a step toward a better society. Others simply wanted a child and had come to feel that skin color wasn't important.

Adoption agencies by then had begun to change their policies. They were willing to place a black child in a white family, although they were careful to counsel the adopting couple about the problems they were likely to run into and to question them closely about their reasons for wanting a black child. Were they using the child to prove how liberal they were? Were they trying to assuage their own feelings of racial guilt? Did they regard a black child as a last resort, or a second or third choice? And what about their relationships with black people in general? Did they have black friends? Were they ready to deal with the discrimination their child was likely to face in the white community?

Many people could answer these questions to the agencies' satisfaction, and by 1972, more than fifteen thousand white families had adopted black children. To many people, this seemed like the simple and logical way to solve two problems at once. Many white families were looking for children to adopt; many black children needed homes. Put families and children together, and both problems were solved. Unfortunately, it wasn't quite that simple. In the early seventies, a controversy began building up about transracial adoption—the placing of a child of one race in a family of another race. The argument focused especially on black children adopted into white families. On both sides were people who had strong feelings and definite opinions about the subject.

Those who favored transracial adoption argued that it's bad for a child to grow up without a family. Children who spend their lives in institutions or in switching from one foster family to another are deprived of something essential—a feeling of being loved and wanted, a feeling of belonging. If a black child can get that feeling from a white family, isn't that better than not getting it at all? And if our goal is to eliminate prejudice and integrate our society, isn't the family a good place to start?

Opponents of transracial adoption, however, brought up other issues. In a racist society such as ours, they said, it's hard enough for black children to feel good about themselves. They need a strong sense of the value of their own history, their own culture, their own beauty as a race. White families can't possibly give them this. Black children growing up in white families will end up with no identity at all. Because of their background, they won't belong to the black community; because of the color of their skin, they won't belong to the white community. They'll be misfits everywhere they go.

In the mid-seventies, a number of black organizations, especially the National Association of Black Social Workers, took a firm stand against transracial adoption, and many individuals agreed with them. "Never in a billion years will any white really know what it's like to be a black!" said one. "So how in the world could white parents give a black child that deep-down knowledge and feeling of blackness?"

The controversy raged fiercely for several years, and it had a strong impact on adoption agencies. They became much more cautious about transracial placements. In fact, by 1976, transracial adoptions had virtually stopped. Instead, many agencies were putting increased efforts into finding black parents to adopt black children. They added black social workers to their staffs. They sent these workers into black neighborhoods to recruit adoptive parents and let them know about adoption agencies in the community.

One such recruiter, who works for a New York agency called Spaulding for Children, speaks to church groups, ministers, and women's groups, goes into bars and pool halls, and talks to people on the streets. He's been a terrific success at finding homes for hard-to-place children.

As for the thousands of black and other minority children who are growing up in white families, it's hard to say for sure what the effects of their experience will be. Most of these children are still fairly young. In five or ten years, when they are adults, they are sure to have interesting things to say. They are the ones who will eventually settle the transracial adoption controversy.

Another kind of transracial adoption has stirred up controversy, too. This is the adoption of children from foreign countries—most often, these days, war orphans from Southeast Asia. In Vietnam orphanages are crammed with homeless children. Some lost their parents when their villages were bombed or burned. Some were brought to the orphanages by sick, wounded, or poverty-stricken parents who could no longer take care of them. Some were simply abandoned and learned to live on the streets, scrounging a living by begging or stealing until they were picked up and taken to some kind of shelter.

Many of these orphans are half Vietnamese and half American, the children of American soldiers, both black and white, and Vietnamese women. Korea, too, has a big population of mixed-race children, leftovers of the American military presence there. In both countries, these children are destined for an especially hard time. They are outcasts in their own societies, victims of a deep racial prejudice. When they're young, they are ignored or tormented by other children. As adults, they will have difficulty finding jobs, friends, and mates. The social pressure frequently drives mothers of mixed-race children to give them up, hoping that they'll be adopted by Americans and grow up where life won't be so cruel to them.

During the Vietnam War, American television began to publicize the plight of these orphans and outcasts. People's hearts were stirred by the sight of them—the thin bodies, the sad, listless faces—and by the knowledge that a great many of them would probably die, since the money and people needed for their care were just not available. Suddenly, letters poured in from families who wanted to adopt these children. Organizations were formed to match children with parents and fly them to this country. Between 1964 and 1975 thousands of American couples found themselves the parents of Vietnamese war orphans.

These parents faced problems that most adoptive parents don't have to deal with. David and Catherine Cupp, for example, adopted a boy named John, who was half Vietnamese and half black. He had spent the first two years of his life on a two- by three-foot wooden shelf in an orphanage, surrounded by flies, dirt, and four hundred other unwanted and undernourished children. Except for a twice daily feeding and diaper changing, John had no real human contact at all. As a result, he was more like a three-month-old infant than a two-year-old child when he came to America. He couldn't walk or even crawl, since he had never done anything but sit on a shelf; he didn't know what his legs were for. One of his ears was infected, and his teeth were decayed. His arms and legs were like sticks, while his body was swollen by malnutrition. His face was stiff and expressionless. He didn't laugh, cry, or smile, no matter what happened to him.

The Cupps had John for six weeks before the first smile broke through his blankness, and it was many months longer before he could walk, talk, and react to things with normal emotions. His new family had to give John a tremendous amount of love and care to make up for the neglect of his early life. But they succeeded. By the age of four, John was healthy at last and was working in nursery school at the same level as other children his age.

Today, adoption of children from foreign countries is more difficult than it was a few years ago. Foreign governments, seeing children as an important national resource, have grown reluctant to part with them. Instead they are increasing their efforts to find homes for them with families in their own countries. Many countries that do allow foreign adoptions have established quotas on it, making just a few babies available to outsiders.

But people who want to adopt can find plenty of children right in this country—for example, handicapped children who live in foster homes, hospitals, and other institutions. Some are severely disabled—paralyzed, blind, afflicted with an incurable disease. Others have mental or emotional problems: they may be extremely retarded or so seriously disturbed that they don't speak or relate to people at all. Few adoptive parents are willing to take on children like these, along with all their problems. In fact, many natural parents, when faced with a newborn child who is in some way defective, shrink from the responsibility and decide to give the child up. (The birth of a handicapped child can also have the opposite effect, however. One woman who had not planned to keep her baby gave birth to a boy who was blind. His blindness, she felt, was a reason *not* to give him up. His especially urgent need for a mother gave her a sense of purpose in caring for him that she had not found in her life before.)

More and more people are realizing that the baby they adopt doesn't have to be "perfect." Many handicapped children can lead nearly normal lives. The child who's had polio and wears a brace on one leg, the child who wears a hearing aid, the child with a heart defect who can't exercise as vigorously as other kids—all were once considered unadoptable. Today they have a much better chance of finding homes.

Of course, the people who adopt hard-to-place children —whether handicapped, older, or minority race—are likely to be rather unusual people, willing to accept extraordinary challenges. Among the most remarkable of these families is that of Dorothy and Bob DeBolt, of Piedmont, California. The DeBolts have nineteen children, and they come from every category of hard-to-place child. Six of the De-Bolts' children are biological: five of them Dorothy's from her first marriage, one Bob's from his. For the rest, the DeBolts are either adoptive parents or legal guardians.

Six of the DeBolts' nonbiological children have handicaps of some kind. Tich and Anh, two Vietnamese boys, were wounded in the war. Karen, a black girl, was born without arms or legs. Sunee and Ly are both crippled by polio. Wendy, who was a battered child, can see out of only one eye, and Twe is totally blind. J.R., a boy who is paralyzed because of a spinal defect, is also blind.

This remarkable family began with Dorothy and her first husband, Ted Atwood. They had five children of their own and two adopted Korean-Caucasian boys. Then Ted died, leaving Dorothy to care for the seven children.

Not long after Ted's death, Dorothy heard about two wounded Vietnamese boys through the Committee of Responsibility, an organization whose purpose was to bring to America children who had been wounded in the war and could not get adequate treatment in Vietnam. Tich had been swimming in a canal when artillery fire tore into his body. His spinal cord was damaged, and the lower half of his body was paralyzed. Anh had stepped on a land mine, which exploded beneath him. He too was paralyzed from the waist down. The boys had had surgery in a California hospital and now needed somewhere to stay while they underwent the long process of rehabilitation.

Taking Tich and Anh into the family would mean dealing with the problems of braces and crutches, infections and pressure sores (from the braces), bowels that couldn't be controlled, hospital visits and therapeutic exercises. Few women in Dorothy's position would even have considered the idea. But the boys needed help, and they had nowhere to go. For Dorothy, those were the decisive facts. She took Tich and Anh home with her.

Bob DeBolt, whom Dorothy met and married soon afterward, shared her feelings about homeless and handicapped children. Together, he and Dorothy added nine more children to the family.

Their household became a scene of constant activity and frequent crisis. But for Dorothy and Bob, the rewards of a family like theirs far outweigh the problems. They've watched Karen, for instance, the child who wears artificial arms and legs, learn after a long struggle to walk down their long flight of stairs. They've seen a dramatic change take place in J.R., the boy who is blind and paralyzed. He came to them depressed and apathetic, resigned to life in a wheelchair. With their help, he mustered all his willpower and learned to walk on crutches. The DeBolts are determined not only to give a home and a family to children who otherwise wouldn't have one but also to teach their handicapped children to be as independent as possible in the outside world.

There are very few families, of course, like the DeBolts —too few to give homes to all the handicapped, older, and minority-race children who have nowhere to go. But a movement is going on to find more such families. Groups of adoptive parents have joined together to provide information and legal advice for others who want to adopt and to give them the support and counseling that families who adopt hard-to-place children often need. These groups also work to change laws that restrict adoptions unnecessarily—those that say adoptive parents must be of the same religion as the child, for example, or that say no single person can adopt.

The North American Council on Adoptable Children, an organization made up of two hundred smaller local groups, is responsible for a real breakthrough in the field of special adoptions. Because of the council's efforts, Congress passed an act that sets up a computerized system called the National Resources Exchange. This is a list of children all over the country who need homes and of parents who want to adopt. With the establishment of this list, thousands of waiting children become for the first time a little less invisible to the people who count most—families with homes to share.

PART II
Views from Inside: The Feelings of Adoption

CHAPTER *4*

The Parents Who Adopt

The telephone rings. The woman answers it, and a voice says, "This is Mrs. Jones of the Children's Home Society. We have a baby for you." The woman's heart starts beating fast. She is so excited she can hardly hear this news she's been waiting for so long. When the conversation is over, she calls her husband immediately. The two of them go to see the baby at the adoption agency the next day, and they bring it home a few days later. Quite suddenly, they have become parents.

Watching them over the next few weeks, no one would know they were any different from other parents. They wash bottles and diapers, they stumble out of bed for midnight feedings, they exclaim in delight every time their baby waggles a finger or blinks an eye. But they are not exactly the same as parents whose children are biological. The years leading up to the baby's arrival were different, and the years that follow will be different, too, in many ways.

Most adoptive parents, though not all, have had to face the fact that they are unable to have their own children. Sometimes the man is infertile; sometimes the woman is. Sometimes doctors can't find any reason for the couple's childlessness, and yet the years go by and no pregnancy occurs. People in this predicament usually feel sad, frustrated, angry, or inadequate—sometimes all of these. If the husband is sterile, the wife may resent him ("If I were married to someone else, I could have my own children"); if the wife is, the husband may feel the same way.

Most people who get married just assume that sooner or later they can have children, if they want to. They look forward to passing on a part of themselves to a child—their musical talent, their curly red hair, or their sense of humor. They want to provide their parents with grandchildren and someday to have grandchildren themselves. And they want to add some new leaves to the family tree and ensure the survival of the family name. People who find out they can't do this are likely to be deeply disappointed.

"I used to cry and cry and cry," said one woman who had tried for years to have a child. "I felt like half a woman, not a whole woman." Men, too, often feel they are not "real men" if they can't father children. The idea that they have somehow failed can make people feel ashamed and embarrassed about their childlessness.

The feeling of grief and loss is even more devastating. Women especially have a hard time with it. Some get terribly depressed when they see other women who are pregnant or who have babies; others get angry and bitter. The time of dealing with childlessness has been likened to a period of mourning. People cry and rage and protest against the injustice of fate, just as they do when someone they love has died.

Some couples are childless for reasons other than infertility. The husband or wife may have, or be a carrier of, a hereditary disease, such as hemophilia or sickle-cell anemia. They might not want to take the risk of having a child who suffers from the same disease. Other couples are prevented from having children by their social conscience: they don't want to bring another child into a seriously overpopulated world when there are plenty of children already here who need good homes.

These people are voluntarily childless. Those who carry an inheritable disease have had less of a choice, but at least they themselves have been the ones to decide against having children, and for clear and compelling reasons. Couples whose childlessness is not their choice at all, however, have a harder time reconciling themselves to it. Some of them carry their grief and anger with them all through their lives; others finally accept their infertility—that is, they stop raging against it and begin to look for a new direction.

For some couples, that means deciding to give up entirely on the idea of having children. They realize that they are whole people even without children and that their marriages can be good and their lives satisfying just as they are. They accept what they can't change and make up their minds to live with it.

Other couples start thinking about adopton. They might look into private adoption, or they might get in touch with an adoption agency. Adoption through an agency has been, for the last thirty years or so, the traditional route, and, although agencies now have far fewer babies available than they used to and many agency policies are being called into question as outdated and inappropriate, this is still the avenue most childless couples try first.

The goal of the social workers at an agency is to find good parents for children who need them. They have guidelines to help them decide which couples will make good parents and which will not. "Raising adopted children is not an ordinary task and not every couple can handle it well," says Linda Burgess, an adoption worker from Washington, D.C. In her twenty years of experience, she interviewed hundreds of couples who wanted to adopt and developed a clear idea of the kind of people she was looking for. "I sought parents who showed enthusiasm, stability, tolerance, and, most of all, ability to grow," she says. "I viewed as negative characteristics tension in their relationships, rigidity, immaturity, sexual incompatibility, and indecisiveness in their commitment to adoption." She also inquired into a couple's reasons for wanting to adopt, and these reasons were often crucial to her decision.

Generally, adoption workers agree on what makes some people better adoptive parents than others. As an example of the agency point of view, imagine a couple we'll call Ralph and Andrea Walker. When they come to the agency, Andrea explains that she is unable to have children and has been unhappy about it. Her unhappiness is so deep and has lasted so long that her relationship with Ralph is suffering. She always seems to feel depressed, distant, or angry. Ralph, worried that their marriage is about to collapse, has suggested that they adopt a child, even though having children is not particularly important to him. So they have come to the agency—Andrea feeling that adopting a child would at least be better than not having one at all, and Ralph hoping that once they have a child Andrea will cheer up and their marriage will get better.

During the interview, Andrea makes it clear that she wants a child who looks as much as possible as if it were hers and Ralph's by birth, and she says that she will accept only a child whose background is "good"—that is, much like her own. Ralph says he hopes they can have a child because Andrea is so miserable without one, which makes her hard to get along with. He doesn't seem very excited about the prospect of being a father, however. He doesn't mention any of his own reasons for wanting a son or daughter.

Most agencies would probably decide that Ralph and Andrea had poor reasons for wanting to adopt. First of all, Andrea was angry and depressed about her inability to have her own children. For her, adoption was not a clear choice but a last resort: it was better than not having a child, and that was about all. Would that feeling come through to her adopted child? the social worker would wonder. She would wonder, too, about Andrea's desire to make sure her adopted child could pass as a biological child. What if the child didn't turn out to look or act like Andrea or Ralph at all? Would Andrea be disappointed—and show it?

The social worker would also be concerned about Ralph's reasons for wanting to adopt. She'd be reluctant to place a child with a couple whose marriage was in trouble, and she'd be worried because Ralph's interest in adopting seemed so much less keen than Andrea's. Most adoption workers look for a husband and wife who both want a child equally and who have a strong relationship with or without children.

The adoption agency would probably reject the Walker's application. They would look more favorably, however, on the application of people like those we'll call the Mendezes —Frank and Marilyn. Marilyn Mendez told the social worker that she had been upset when she found she could not have children. But her "mourning period" was now over, she said, and both she and Frank realized that what they really wanted was the experience of raising, caring for, and loving a child. They were not concerned that the child be a small replica of themselves; they were both active, athletic people avid campers and tennis players, but if their child turned out to like playing the violin or tinkering with cars, that would be fine with them. What they wanted was the chance to become a family, with all the pleasures and problems that go with it.

The Mendezes want to adopt in order to share what they have with a child, not because they expect a child to solve their problems or fill the gaps in their life. This is an attitude that agencies look for in adoptive parents, along with others such as a willingness to speak openly about the adoption with the child and other members of the family and a willingness to accept a child who is different from them. If the Mendezes can show that they possess these qualities, their application is likely to be accepted.

The purpose of this kind of screening is to provide children with the best possible parents, and often it does so. But critics of the agencies say that the selection process can also be unfair. They resent the agencies' power to "play God" with sometimes desperate couples, deciding who is fit to be a parent and who isn't on the basis of subjective standards. One couple might be turned down because of personality differences between them and the social worker or because they were nervous or intimidated by the interview questions. Another couple might be accepted because they had studied beforehand the "correct" answers to the questions they could expect to be asked. Many couples feel that it's degrading to be grilled by adoption workers on intimate aspects of their lives. They are likely to be emotionally upset to begin with, having just come through a period of mourning for their childlessness; the process of adoption, under these circumstances, can be not only painful but damaging to their self-esteem.

Until now, however, no foolproof method of determining who will make good parents and who won't has been devised. Some kind of screening is necessary for the child's protection, but it has to be done by a person, not a machine, and that means it's bound to have flaws. Linda Burgess, the adoption worker quoted earlier, calls adoption an art. Unlike the decisions of science, which are based completely on facts, the decisions of adoption must be based on feelings and intuitions as well. They will never be perfect, but they can, at their best, be as good as humanly possible.

Once two people have decided to adopt and have applied for and received their baby, they become more or less indistinguishable from any other set of parents. They can take the attitude that they are, in fact, exactly like a biological family and act as if that were true. Or they can acknowledge that they are not quite the same and never will be. Psychologists, social workers, and adoptive parents have debated for years about which attitude makes for happier family relationships. Today they generally agree with sociologist David Kirk, who believes that in a family where the difference is acknowledged there is more trust and better communication.

One thing that makes it difficult for adoptive parents to think of their families as identical to biological families is that the community around them doesn't think that way. No matter how completely parents accept an adopted child as their own, in the eyes of other people a child by adoption is different from a child by birth. Adoptive parents are reminded of this often.

Grandparents, for example, are sometimes slow to accept an adopted child. They may have had their hearts set on a grandchild in whom they'd be able to see a resemblance to Great-aunt Harriet and who would grow up with the same talent for business as Grandpa Randolph. They may be disappointed when no such grandchild appears and unable to see an adopted child as an acceptable substitute. Usually they come to love their adopted grandchildren in spite of themselves, but some grandparents can never really accept an adopted child as part of the family in the same way as a birth child. This can show up right at the beginning if, for example, the parents want to name the new baby after an ancestor and the grandparents object, saying the baby is not really "of their blood." Or it can show up much later, when it comes time to pass on family heirlooms and grandparents have a hard time seeing adopted children as legitimate heirs.

The adoptive parents' friends can also make them feel their difference, often inadvertently. Well-meaning remarks, like "Polly looks so much like you that she might be your own" or "You really are wonderful people for taking in this child," remind adoptive parents that they are not quite the same as other parents. Sometimes the remarks of acquaintances or strangers can be ignorant, tactless, and hurtful. David Kirk, an adoptive father himself, recalled a time when he and his wife were waiting anxiously in the hospital while their daughter was having her tonsils out. Someone they knew walked by and, learning why the Kirks were there, said to Mrs. Kirk, "Why, that's just like a real mother!"

An adoptive mother is a real mother, and an adoptive father is a real father. The fact that they have adopted their child doesn't mean they will do any less or feel any less for that child than birth parents would. It's just that adoptive parents have things to deal with in the parent-child relationship that birth parents don't.

One of these things is an awareness that their children's characteristics didn't all come from them. Their children inherited their looks and some of their talents and personality traits from other people. If a nonadopted child displays a wonderful ability to draw, his mother can say, "He gets that from Aunt Minnie, who painted such beautiful pictures." If a nonadopted child explodes into terrible temper tantrums, her father can say, "She's just like me that way." But the unexpected traits and talents of an adopted child can't be matched up like that and made into evidence that the child belongs to the family. Instead, these traits are evidence that the child has another family as well.

Most adoptive parents have a slightly uneasy feeling about this other family. Part of their uneasiness comes from what they know. Perhaps the adoption agency has told them that their child's mother was an unmarried fourteen-year-old of Irish heritage, from a Catholic family, and that the father was an unemployed eighteen-year-old. That's all the information they have. They have no idea what their child's parents were like as people, what their personalities were like or their interests or abilities. Often they choose to shut these other parents out of their minds. The child, after all, will be growing up in their family and will learn his or her ways from them. But they can't forget about the birth parents altogether, especially when traits that are probably inherited show up in their child.

Some adoptive parents are afraid of what their child may have inherited from this unknown background. They worry that the child has "bad blood," that the birth parents, who might have had what the adoptive parents consider undesirable characteristics, have passed these characteristics on. If their child turns out to be difficult and rebellious, they are apt to say, "That comes from the birth parents, not from us."

Other parents are just bewildered by their child's unexpected differences from them. Adoption worker Linda Burgess describes a boy named George who asked for piano lessons when he was fifteen and displayed an amazing talent as soon as he started. His adoptive parents had no particular musical abilities, but his grandmother by birth had been a concert pianist.

The adoptive parents of a boy named Tom were calm, steady people, easy-going and even-tempered. Tom, however, was anxious, tense, impatient, and unpredictable. His parents were puzzled by him and worried that they might be doing something wrong. When they were able to look at the file on Tom's birth parents, they learned that both his mother and his father had been "high-strung individuals." Tom was probably, by birth, just a different kind of person from his adoptive parents.

It appears that the general inclination of a person's personality can be inherited—that is, you can be born with a tendency to be an outgoing, social kind of person or a quiet, solitary one or a restless and independent one. It also seems that you can inherit talents and aptitudes. (Burgess mentions, for example, an adopted boy who discovered as a teenager that he loved sailing. Though he didn't know it, his birth ancestors had been sailors for five generations.) But you don't inherit a specific program for your life—only a tendency in one direction or another. If an adopted girl's birth mother was an unmarried fourteen-year-old, that doesn't mean that the girl herself is likely to have a baby at fourteen. If an adopted boy's birth father served time in jail, that doesn't mean the boy ever will. The idea that "bad blood" will somehow show up in ways like these is old-fashioned and inaccurate.

Adoption agencies have some ways of guarding against the problems that arise because of adoptive parents' attitudes toward their child's heritage. They make an effort, for example, to avoid placing a child with parents who are likely to have strong negative feelings about some aspects of the child's background. Some people, for instance, disapprove strongly of drinking. If they adopted a child whose birth mother had been an alcoholic, they might hold that against the child, perhaps without even being aware they were doing so. Or, when the child became a teenager and tried his first beer, they might be consumed by the groundless fear that he too was bound to become an alcoholic. The agency, foreseeing these possibilities, would probably not place that child with those parents.

But agencies can't ensure that differences between adopted children and their parents won't arise or that these differences will be easy to deal with. Parents who wish to forget about the original mother and father and mold their child into what they think a child of theirs ought to be are likely to have trouble. "Grown adopted children know full well that their adoptive heritage is not their own," says Linda Burgess. "They come to feel like outsiders in families where ancestor worship and class snobbery pervade. Those who are very unlike their adopters may have a particularly strong sense of not belonging. There is only one course for parents to take: open discussion of true heritage and acceptance of differences between their children and themselves."

Such open discussions, however, can be hard for adoptive parents. They are uncomfortable talking about that other set of parents, frightened that bringing them out into the open might somehow make them too real to the child, more the "real parents" than they are themselves. It would be so much easier if those other parents could be completely ignored.

In the past, many adoptive parents tried to do just that. A woman adopting a baby might leave home for several months and come back with a child she claimed to have given birth to. Some women even wore increasingly large pillows under their clothes for nine months to convince others that the babies they brought home were their own. Then they would act exactly as if this were true, keeping the child's adoption a deep secret, especially from the child.

No one knows, of course, how many adopted children grew up and lived out their lives without once suspecting that they were adopted. But certainly a large number suspected it or found out accidentally. Some found out suddenly, through relatives' slips of the tongue or by going through papers after their parents had died; others became convinced of it intuitively over the years, feeling that they were different from their parents or that something was being hidden from them. Either way, such a revelation is likely to be accompanied by a feeling of having been deceived.

Other parents did tell their children that they had been adopted, but cut off any further discussion of the subject by saying that the original parents had both died (usually in a plane crash or a car accident) and that nothing more about them was known. Again, some people probably believed this all their lives. Others questioned it, found out it wasn't true, and felt betrayed and angry.

These days, few parents keep their child's adoption a secret. In fact, agencies usually insist that parents agree beforehand to be open about adoption with their children. This puts the parents, though, in a position that some have called the "double bind" of adoption: they are supposed to make the child their own and at the same time tell him he isn't. It calls up all those uneasy questions that may be lurking in the parents' minds: "Are we really the *real* parents? Is our child going to feel that those other parents are 'realer' than we are? Is he going to feel rejected because they gave him away?"

In spite of these fears, however, nearly all adoptive parents today resolve to tell their children. The question is when to tell and what to say. About this there's a lot of disagreement.

According to one school of thought, it's best to tell the child early. The idea is that a child who grows up in a family where the word "adopted" is common and familiar won't make a big deal out of it. Adoption will be just another aspect of the child's life. "We introduced the word 'adoption' at the age of one," said one parent, "along with 'mommy,' 'daddy,' 'cat,' and 'dog.' "

Other people advocate waiting until the child is old enough to understand and has a personality well developed enough to handle the news. Psychologist Herbert Weider thinks that for children younger than six the half-understood knowledge may be a burden. Another therapist, Marshall Schecter, says, "I would prefer children being told by parents at a time when the communication system is open and good feelings abound. This is usually between seven and ten."

Both approaches have their drawbacks. Some parents who introduce the word "adoption" right away may overemphasize it, using it so often in an attempt to be open that they succeed only in making the child feel different from everyone else. Parents who wait until later run the risk of losing some of the child's trust when he finds out he has been kept in the dark until then. Betty Jean Lifton, a writer who was an adopted child herself, says, "What is important is that there should not be a dogmatic attitude about the age the child is told. One should belong to neither the 'tell early' nor the 'tell later' school, but should decide what is best for the needs of one's own family."

What Lifton and many others advocate is to tell children when they ask to be told. At the age of three or four, a child may ask something like this: "Mommy, why is Aunt Martha's tummy so fat?" or "Where did Larry get his baby sister?" This shows that she's ready for at least the basic information about where babies come from. At this point, the mother may say, "Some babies grow inside their mothers, and others come from the adoption agency. That's where we got you." For a while, the child may be perfectly happy with that explanation. Later on, though, other questions will begin to occur to her. She may wonder why she didn't come from inside her mother. She may wonder whom she did come from and where that person is now. As she asks questions, her parents provide answers.

But what answers? What to tell is just as difficult and controversial as when to tell. Many adoptive parents tell some version of the "chosen-child" story. They talk about going to the agency and walking through rooms full of babies, looking closely at all of them, until they came to the one they knew immediately was the one for them. "We chose you," they will say. "Other babies just come to their parents, and they have to take them, whether they like them or not. But we picked you because we liked you best. You're special." Some parents make the story dramatic and suspenseful and let the child participate in it. A parent might end such a story by asking, "And who do you think that special baby was, the one we picked from all the others?" And the child can answer, "That was me—Billy!" The child may love the story and ask to hear it over and over.

Some people feel, however, that the chosen-child story can put a burden on a young child. If Billy was specially chosen because he was so wonderful, doesn't he have to live up to that specialness and continue to be wonderful? He may worry that if he turns out not to be so wonderful, his parents will be sorry they picked him or might even take him back where he came from, unlike other parents, who have to take whatever kind of baby they get.

Also, the chosen-baby story usually leaves out a crucial element—Billy's birth mother. The adoptive parents may include her by saying, "She wasn't able to take care of you, but she loved you very much and wanted you to have a good home. That's why she took you to the adoption agency, where we got you." But the typical story makes it sound as if the child somehow originated at the adoption agency. Parents who are otherwise open about their child's adoption may clam up when it comes to the subject of the birth parents. If the child asks questions, they reply that they don't know the answers, which is often true, since adoption agencies don't usually provide much background information. But even if parents do know some facts, they may be reluctant to reveal them. "We know very little," one parent said, "that her parents weren't married, that her mother went to college. But I would never want to tell her those things because it would make the mother more real, and I guess I would never want to do that."

The trouble is that the birth mother *is* real and probably won't disappear from the child's mind just because she's never talked about. Silence and evasion, in fact, may make the child think there's something wrong with her origins and, consequently, wrong with herself.

The alternative is to tell the child what really happened.

This can be hard, of course, not only for the parents but for the child. At the heart of adoption is a difficult truth: the child's original parents chose not to keep him. Adoptive parents are afraid that telling the child will upset him, and perhaps harm him emotionally. Some therapists and social workers, however, are beginning to think the opposite: that the harm comes from *not* knowing, from the cloud of mystery and silence and uneasiness that the child senses around the subject of his first parents.

That doesn't mean that a four-year-old needs to be told the entire history of his birth. He is too young to understand things like social pressures, economic hardships, and difficult decisions. But as he grows older and continues to ask questions, he can be told more and more, until finally, by the time he is perhaps eighteen, he knows all that his parents know about his other family.

Even those who favor this approach don't say it will be easy. It requires both parents and children to face an unsettling fact: that they do not belong together by blood, that they are different from other families. But while bringing up this issue and discussing it may be the most difficult thing to do, it is also the most honest. It keeps the channels of communication open between parents and children instead of making the one crucial subject seem dark and somehow threatening. It avoids deception by the parents and later feelings of betrayal by the child. And it implies a trust between parents and children—the parents' trust that the child is strong enough to handle the facts of his origin and that he will continue to love them even after he knows it, and the child's trust that his parents will not lie to him and that they will respect his special identity. For the truth is that that special identity is part of an adopted child's life, and there is nothing the adoptive parents can do to change it.

CHAPTER 5

The Adopted Children

How does it feel to be adopted? "I was grateful to have been adopted," says one adoptee. "I considered myself special."

"Adoption colored my whole life," says another. "I have always felt rejected and worthless."

Two opposite experiences, and yet these people are alike in at least one way: being adopted made a difference in their lives.

Adopted people have only recently begun to talk about this. In the past, a conspiracy of silence surrounded the whole subject of adoption. Since adoptive families were supposed to be just like other families, adopted children usually tried to squash down any disturbing feelings of being different.

Today, however, things are changing. Adopted people are getting together in groups to talk about their feelings. They are writing down their experiences in books and magazine articles. They are forming organizations to study adoption and its effects. And the more they talk and write and study, the more they realize that being adopted has set them apart in some ways from other people.

Every adoptee's experience, of course, is different. But as more and more adopted people tell their stories, they're realizing how similar these stories often are. As children, feeling different from other people but not talking about that feeling, they thought themselves alone in the world, as though they spoke a foreign language that no one could quite understand. Now, as grown people sharing their histories, they've suddenly found thousands of others who understand perfectly well. There is something that might be called "the adoption experience" that ties them all together.

It often begins with the chosen-baby story. Many adoptees have some variation of it in their memories. The elements of the story are generally similar: the parents longing for a baby, the room full of cribs, the wonderful baby they recognize instantly as theirs, the specialness of being chosen rather than just arriving; it's all designed to make the child feel good. But it doesn't always have that effect.

"During my childhood I used to brag about being chosen," said one adoptee, "but when I was a little older I started to wonder what it all meant and why my birth mother hadn't wanted me. I feel the chosen-baby story really backfired because I felt or sensed that they were overcompensating."

Another adoptee expressed similar feelings: "I was told I was adopted from the very beginning, but I felt that my parents overdid it by introducing me as 'our specially chosen adopted daughter.' This always embarrassed me, as it drew attention to my being adopted."

"I didn't want to be adopted or special," another person said. "I just wanted to be ordinary."

Most kids *do* want to be ordinary; that's the trouble. Few girls want to wear lacy dresses when all their friends are wearing jeans; few boys are happy as the only kid with a crewcut when everyone else has long hair. The same kind of feeling—which can be especially strong in teenagers—applies to being adopted. Given a choice between being "chosen and special" or being just like everyone else, most adoptees would probably choose the latter.

To be adopted is to have a different history from most people, one that's full of question marks. Who were my first parents? the adopted child wonders. Why did they give me up? Was there something wrong with me? Was there something wrong with them? The facts are hidden away, and it's easy to believe that they're hidden because they're ugly.

Many adoptees turn their suspicions first on themselves. When they get old enough to look beyond the chosen-baby story, they encounter an undeniable fact: they were born to mothers who gave them away. How could any mother do that? they wonder. To be rejected by its mother, a child would have to be exceptionally unlovable.

Adoptive parents may reinforce this idea without meaning to. When little Bobby asks, "Why did my first mother give me away?" his mother may back away from the subject by giving an abrupt or evasive answer. She may say, "I don't know," or "The agency never told us," simply because she doesn't want to make Bobby's "other mother" into a real person in his mind. Bobby will get a clear message— "I don't want to talk about that"—but won't understand that his mother is feeling threatened or is trying to protect him. He is likely to think instead that his mother knows the answer and won't tell. And the reason she won't tell, he figures, is that his first mother gave him away because there was something wrong with him.

Or it might have been because there was something wrong with *her*. A mother who gives away her baby is a bad mother, isn't she? And if his parents refuse to talk about her, it must be because she was not a good person. Unfortunately, this line of reasoning brings Bobby back once again to himself. If the mother who bore him was a bad person, then probably he is, too.

The feeling that they were unwanted sometimes comes out in adopted children as a fear of being lost or abandoned. One adoptee said, "As I was growing up I had an overwhelming fear of being left or forgotten and becoming lost. If I was taken some place, Sunday school, dancing lessons, or the movies, and someone was to come for me, I was terrified they would forget about me and not come." It's as though the adopted child is thinking, "If my first parents left me, why couldn't it happen again?"

Some adopted children, however, have parents who are careful to be reassuring. When a child asks why she was given up, they tell her that her first mother wanted very much to keep her but could not; that the mother loved her and wanted her to have the kind of family that she couldn't provide, that the mother gave her up because she *did* love her, not because she didn't. According to social workers who work with birth mothers, this is the truth in the vast majority of cases. To the child who looks at it a certain way, though, it's the opposite of reassuring. If her first mother gave her away because she couldn't take care of her, what would happen if her new parents suddenly lost all their money or became ill? Would they also give her away because they couldn't take care of her?

Even when the family does everything possible to assure the child that she is all right, that her mother was all right, and that being adopted is all right, people outside the family may communicate something different.

"Illegitimate," for example, is the way society describes a child born to an unmarried mother, as most adopted children were. It's a term that has lost a lot of its power in recent years; most people no longer think less of someone just because he or she was born out of wedlock. Nevertheless, the word "illegitimate" is still in use, and adopted people sometimes find themselves labeled with it: "You're adopted? Oh, then you must have been an illegitimate child." Built into the word is the implication that other people are somehow right and proper in a way that the child born out of wedlock is not.

As young children, adoptees are especially vulnerable to

this kind of social attitude. Other kids may fling "adopted" at them like a bad word, and they will take it that way, not yet having the understanding and self-confidence to shrug it off. No matter how loving and reassuring their adoptive parents are, it's hard for adoptees not to feel a twinge of uncertainty when their friends say, "Those aren't your *real* parents," or "How come no one wanted you when you were born?" or "A mother who gives away her own baby is no good."

So families, friends, and society in general continue to remind children that they are adopted. Adoption makes them different. It's not necessarily either a bad difference or a good difference, but usually it's one that children are aware of and that they struggle to come to terms with throughout their lives.

What they worry about and want to know depends a great deal on how old they are. A seven-year-old's concerns are not the same as an eighteen-year-old's. Very young children are quite absorbed in themselves. When they learn about adoption, they're likely to ask about their own infant selves—whether they were big or little, for instance, or whether or not they were pretty babies. When they get a little older, the idea of the "other mother" becomes more interesting. They ask, "What did she look like? What is her name? Where is she now?" They're apt to get unsatisfactory answers; their parents either don't know or don't want to talk about it. So the mystery stays with them, and though they may stop asking questions they continue to wonder.

Since they have no facts, they often turn to fantasy. Many adoptees report having spent long childhood hours imagining what their biological mother might have been like. "I envisioned my mother as having a large brood of kids and being too poor to help me," said one person.

"I dreamed of my birth mother as a fairy godmother," said another, "someone who was young and beautiful."

"I had the usual dreams and fantasies that I was the son of a glamorous, wealthy woman who would come and take me away on a white horse."

Fantasies like these can be especially powerful when children are angry with their adoptive parents. "My *real* mother wouldn't treat me this way," the child thinks. "My real mother would be nicer"—or prettier, or richer, or smarter. Children who *aren't* adopted also imagine sometimes that they don't really belong with the parents they have and that their real parents, from whom they were somehow separated at birth, are far more grand or glamorous. Soon, however, the nonadopted child gives up this idea, since all the evidence is against it (pictures of the child as an infant, for instance, and resemblances between the child and other members of the family). The adopted child does not give it up. The truth is, the adoptee *does* have other parents, and whatever the child imagines about them *could* be true.

The main feelings of the young child (between seven and ten) mulling over adoption are likely to be curiosity (sometimes mild, sometimes intense) and a kind of storybook romanticizing (the birth mother as either beautiful and glamorous or mean and poor). As children get older, however, their questions and fantasies change. For teenagers, the mystery of their origins takes on a whole new significance.

Adolescence is the time when people begin to put together their identities—that is, to figure out who they are. Usually, a person's identity is complex. It's a little like a painting, made up of many different strokes and colors that add up to a complete picture. In this case, the whole picture is made up of all the different aspects of a person's self—physical, psychological, social, religious, racial, national, and so on. One person, for example, might describe himself like this: "I am a shy, quiet guy with some talent in art. I'm the tall, skinny type, not ugly but not great-looking, either. I come from an ordinary middle-class family, English background on one side and French on the other. My parents are Episcopalian, but I'm not. I don't believe in any religion." Someone else's identity might focus on different kinds of things: "I'm the sort of person who prefers actions to words. I'm interested in politics; I like to get involved and make changes. As a black person and a woman I care about my rights. I come from a family of hardworking, determined people, and that's the way I am, too."

Your identity connects you to other people. You identify with the people of a certain race or nationality and with people who believe a certain way and with people of a certain social and educational level. When you're with them, you feel as if you belong. You have a clear sense of how you fit into the world around you because you have a clear sense of who you are.

Of course, you don't just make up your identity out of thin air. Some of it is handed to you at birth—your race, for example, your nationality, your physical appearance, and your inborn traits and potentials. And a large part is determined by your parents. They live in Alabama or New York; they have a lot of money or a little; they are activists for the radical left or fundamentalist Baptists or eccentric artists; they are nervous or easy-going, loving or distant. Whether you embrace their ways as your own or rebel against them, they will inevitably shape who you are.

Adopted people, when they start to think about who they are, run into a puzzle here. On the one hand, they are the children of their adoptive parents; on the other hand, they are the children of two unknowns. They don't know their national origins; they don't know who their ancestors were; they've never seen other people who look like them. And so to some degree the identity of an adopted person remains incomplete.

How important is that incompleteness? Some people

say not very. After all, an adopted person, from the mo
ment he or she was adopted, has been a full-fledged
member of a family and has a group of people and a way
of life to identify with just like everyone else. Some adopted
people feel this way. They identify with the life their
adoptive parents have given them and don't feel that who
their birth parents were makes any difference at all.

To other adoptees it does make a difference. That gap
in their identity is important and troubling to them. Researchers who have studied the problems of adoptees call
what they are feeling "genealogical bewilderment," and
they see this as a normal consequence of being adopted.
They point out that most people take their family connection for granted. They talk casually about how the new
baby looks just like Aunt Carrie, and how Jim gets his
singing voice from Uncle Bill; they make remarks like this:
"Our family is mostly Italian, except for one English great-
grandmother," or "In our family, in the past most of the
men have been doctors, and the women have been teach-
ers," or "My family has lived in California for five generations." But they often don't realize how central it is to their
identities to have this feeling of connection with a long
line of people.

One aspect of genealogical bewilderment is physical.
Nonadopted children look around them and see other people with the came color eyes, the same curly hair, the
same allergics, the same weight problems. This helps them
to form a "body image"—a picture of themselves that's not
limited to what they see in the mirror. They know where
their physical characteristics came from and how they are
likely to change as years pass.

Adopted children don't have this background knowledge,
and they miss it, especially those who look markedly different from their adoptive families. Many adoptees, when
talking about themselves, mention how much they feel
this lack. "I had a feeling of oneness," said one person. "I

was the only tall brunette in a family of short, blue-eyed blondes."

"I used to cry and look at myself in the mirror and wonder if my mother looked like me," said another. Poring over magazines and newspapers for pictures of people they resemble and staring at faces on the street wondering, "Could that be my mother, my brother, my sister?" are common adoptee pastimes.

But adoptees also feel a disconnectedness that is more than physical. It has to do with the lack of a family tradition they feel is their own. Who are "their own people"? Adoptees either don't know or have only a small amount of information on which to base guesses. As young children, they may imagine their birth parents were kings and queens or movie stars; as teenagers, however, they are more aware of social and sexual realities and are likely to picture birth mothers as prostitutes and loose women and fathers as irresponsible playboys. They are learning from their adoptive parents that having indiscriminate sexual relations and having babies out of wedlock are improper things to do and that the people who do them are immature, irresponsible, and even immoral. Adopted teenagers may perhaps assume that their birth parents were just such people. That means that their own family traditions and "their own people" are not the kind to inspire much pride.

So adoptees may feel there's a stain on them somehow, as though part of the answer to the question "Who am I?" is unsavory or scary. They wonder if the ways of their birth parents will show up in them; they think about marrying and having children and wonder what heritage they will be passing on.

All these doubts and questions can make the adopted child's teenage years unusually turbulent. Parents and teenagers often have a hard time understanding each other anyway. Adoption can complicate things. If the parents, too, are worried about the child's genetic background, then child and parents will aggravate each other's fear, with unfortunate results for both.

Suppose, for example, that the Greens are the adoptive parents of a daughter named Janice. All they know about her birth parents is that they were both very young. Janice is now fifteen. She is restless and independent, eager to explore life. And she's popular: her friends include as many boys as girls, and she's been dating for over a year. Now she has a fairly serious boyfriend, whom she's been seeing for several months.

Janice's parents want to protect her. They worry that her social life may get in the way of her studies; they worry that she'll get too serious about her boyfriend; they worry that she'll become sexually active and run the risk of getting pregnant. To some extent, all parents of teenage girls worry about these things. But for Janice's parents, there's an added dimension: they know that Janice's birth mother actually did the very things they are worried about.

So, because of their fear that Janice may take after her mother, they are more protective than other parents. In fact, they are downright restrictive. They are suspicious of Janice's friends; they grill her about her activities; they lay down strict rules and regulations.

Janice finds their attitude oppressive. She and her parents have constant arguments. She often defies the rules and does what she wants. And she deeply resents what she sees as their lack of trust in her. She knows they're afraid she'll turn out to be just like her mother; she's a little afraid of it, too. But all their fears and rules, instead of keeping her safely away from her mother's fate, seem instead to push her toward it. Since her parents are sure she's going to go out and get pregnant anyway, why not just go ahead and do it? Since they're treating her as if she's a tramp, maybe she should just be one.

Some girls in Janice's position rebel in exactly this way. They live out their parents' fears and their own fears, connecting themselves to what they think is their true family tradition by carrying it on. In many cases, however, what they imagine about their birth parents is quite wrong. If Janice, for example, had been able to see her mother as a naive and vulnerable girl caught in a net of circumstances and trying to do the right thing, instead of as a wild and heedless tramp, she might have felt differently—and acted differently as well.

Not all adopted teenagers rebel, of course. In fact, many carefully stamp down their curiosity about their birth parents and their own feelings of incomplete identity because they can see how much their questions upset their adoptive parents. The message they get, whether their parents actually come out and say it or not, is "If you really loved us, you wouldn't care about those other people. You wouldn't ask these hurtful, ungrateful questions." And so they keep their questions to themselves. Their curiosity stays with them, but it's tinged with guilt, since they've learned that wanting to know about your birth parents is exactly the same as rejecting your adoptive parents. Some adoptees have spent years feeling like bad, unworthy sons and daughters because they could never quite dismiss the mystery of their origins from their minds.

Some psychologists believe that the stresses of being adopted—the feelings of being different, of not belonging, the sense of not quite knowing who they are—make adoptees more likely than other people to have psychological problems. Researchers have come up with figures that seem to show a high proportion of adopted people among those who come to mental health clinics for help. Some articles claim that adopted children are less likely than other children to live up to their potential in school and more likely to lack self-confidence and independence. None of these figures and studies has proved anything conclusively, however. On the other side of the issue are researchers who advance their own evidence to show that adopted children are no more susceptible to problems than anyone else.

Children who do have problems because they're adopted usually come from families in which the subject of adoption is either taboo or surrounded by uneasy feelings. Some parents try to keep their children's adoption a complete secret. When the children eventually find out about it—as they nearly always do—the shock can be deeply disturbing.

A boy named Greg, for example, had no suspicion that he was adopted until he was seventeen. He and his younger brother got into a fight, and just as Greg was about to hit him, his grandmother cried, "Don't touch that child! He's theirs! You're not!" In that way, Greg found out that he was adopted, while his brother was his parents' biological child. He describes himself as "an emotional basket case" after that. Suddenly, he didn't know who he was at all. He drifted into a pattern of lying and using drugs. It took him years to put himself back together again.

Many adoptees who find out unexpectedly have the kind of violent reaction Greg did. They feel as if the ground has suddenly disappeared from beneath their feet. Those who know they're adopted all along don't have such a shock to deal with, but many of them describe feelings that can be just as damaging: "I've always had a terrible sense of helplessness and hopelessness," says one person. Others talk about feeling worthless and rejected, or isolated and misunderstood.

And still others have none of these feelings. They have felt not only loved but understood by their parents; they have accepted that being adopted makes them different in some ways but no better or worse than other people. (Gary, whose story began this book, is someone like that.)

But even so, many healthy and happy adoptees from open and loving families describe a kind of background awareness of being adopted that is always with them—"a constant gnawing that never goes away," as one person said. The missing family connection is like a dark spot, or a blank spot, in their otherwise full lives.

Some people learn to ignore that spot. They resign themselves to the fact that part of their history is lost to them and decide that it makes no difference. Other people are not resigned. Their need to answer the question "Who am I?" is overwhelmingly strong. Adoptee discussion groups and books and articles about adoptees' experiences make it easier than it used to be for those people to explore their feelings. There's even an organization specifically for adopted teenagers, the Adoptee Pen Pal Club, started by Betty Jean Lifton through *Seventeen* magazine in 1977. Teenagers who want to correspond with other adoptees can write to her in care of *Seventeen*, 850 Third Avenue, New York, New York 10022.

Talking or writing to others whose lives have been like theirs gives adoptees a valuable sense of connection. But even that may not be enough. Some still find the blank spot in their lives intolerable. They can't be at peace until they know the missing first chapter of their history. They can't feel whole until they find out where they came from. They are the ones who decide to search for the parents who gave them birth.

PART **III**

Rights in Conflict: The Issues of Adoption

CHAPTER **6**

The
Searchers

Adopted people who want to meet their birth parents can't just go to a telephone book and look them up. They don't know where their parents live or even what their names are. To find out, they have to set out on a search that can be as complicated as a detective story and just as full of fear, suspense, devastating setbacks, and amazing revelations.

Adopted people who set out to find their birth parents are likely to be fiercely determined about it. They have to be, because the countless roadblocks that arise in the searcher's path are enough to discourage all but the most persistent. Even deciding to search is not easy. In the past especially, adoptees were often told that curiosity about their birth parents was not normal. It was a sign that they themselves were seriously confused, said the psychologists and social workers. Instead of looking for their parents, they ought to be looking for a good psychiatrist.

Plenty of adopted people feel this way themselves; they believe that searching is unnecessary and childish and that people who do it are living in a fantasy world instead of getting on with real life. Because of this, adoptees who do want to search may still have trouble making the actual decision. They are often plagued by self-doubt. Am I normal? they wonder. Is my need to know my birth parents just a symptom of some disturbance, or is it real?

Another stumbling block is guilt toward adoptive parents. It's common for adoptees to feel that their need to know their birth parents is somehow a slap in the face to the parents who raised them, especially when their adoptive parents feel this way, too. It's hard to feel all right about being curious if the very mention of your birth parents hurts or angers your adoptive parents. People outside the family can reinforce this guilt. One of the first adoptees to search for her birth parents and describe her search in a book was a woman named Florence Fisher. In a hospital where she went to find some of her records, she encountered a woman who said to her, "Don't you feel that your obligations are to your adoptive parents? Don't you owe your loyalty to the people who took you, raised you, fed you, cared for you . . . Dwell on the fact that you should be eternally grateful and on the terrible fate that would surely have befallen you had these good people not taken you into their home."

Sometimes adoptees who want to find their birth parents put off the search until their adoptive parents have died; others go ahead with it but keep it completely secret. They are afraid that if they admit what they're doing, their adoptive parents will see it as a betrayal, and they will lose their family's love. Usually, that's the last thing they want to do.

They also fear what their search may reveal. What if the birth parents are dead? What if they are people the searcher doesn't like or feels ashamed of? What if they say, "Go away, don't bother me, I don't want to see you"? Thinking about the possibilities, adoptees hesitate to begin the search.

If they do begin, they are faced immediately with still another barrier: the adoption records are sealed. They know little if anything about their birth parents—probably not even their names—and it is illegal for agencies to allow them to see their files. How in the world will they go about finding two complete unknowns?

Searching for your birth parents, as one adoptee described it, is like "opening a dark and frightening tunnel that might have no end." And the tunnel is lined with hazards—both inner ones, like guilt and apprehension, and outer ones, like adoption laws and agency policies.

Nevertheless, people search. If you ask them why, you'll hear a similarity in their answers. They talk about wanting to complete their identities, to become whole; they talk of their need to know.

"About the fact of looking I had no doubts: I had to look. There was something about me that I didn't know," wrote Florence Fisher.

"Even though you have wonderful folks and live in a loving home," said another adoptee, "no one can convince me that an adopted child will not always have a yearning to know just who he really is."

One adopted woman compares a person's life to a jigsaw puzzle "with bits and pieces fitting together to make it complete—except for the adopted child there are pieces missing. The only explanation he gets is that they just aren't there. For most of us, this is just not adequate. We, too, long to be whole."

"Isn't it natural for me to wonder about my past?" asks someone else. "I feel that it couldn't harm me to know. . . . I have the need to know."

It's the strength of this need that pushes adoptees beyond the fear and guilt and into the search. Most often, they look for their birth mothers; fathers, if they are searched for at all, are usually the second step. The searchers themselves seem to be women more often than men— perhaps because women, being the childbearers, are more concerned with matters of heredity and perhaps also because the realm of feelings, family, and personal relationships is generally more important for women than for men.

According to some researchers, adoptees who search for their birth parents are most likely to be those whose relationship with their adoptive parents was poor. Other people's findings differ. One research team studied fifty adoptees who searched for their birth parents and found that most of them had a fairly good relationship with their adoptive parents. "The desire for genealogical background information is probably shared by all adoptees," this team concluded, "but interest in the birth parents can become a burning issue for some, simply because they have curious minds and approach all life's mysteries in an inquisitive manner. Their search is not necessarily related to the quality of the adoptive relationship."

Adoptees arrive at their decision to search by different roads. For some, the desire grows slowly over many years, beginning as curiosity and ending as definite need. For others, the desire to search is triggered by some event in their lives. Becoming pregnant or having a child, for example, can have that effect on an adopted woman. "Giving birth to a baby wasn't just a minor event," one woman said. "I suddenly realized it was an experience that changes and shapes a woman's life. I felt very cheated that I had never known my natural mother. I guess after my daughter was born I started to identify with my mother and felt a strong desire to know her."

Becoming ill can also plunge an adoptee into the search. Family medical history can sometimes be crucial to the treatment of a person's illness. Jerry Hulse, in a book called *Jody*, describes a case like this. His wife, who had been an adopted child, was rushed to the hospital in critical condition when an artery leading to her brain was blocked. Whether the doctor decided on one treatment or another depended on information that only a blood relative could provide, and so Hulse embarked on a desperate—and luckily, successful—search for his wife's birth mother.

Less urgent medical situations can also send adoptees off on the search. Some people want to know if there are any hereditary diseases in the family that could be passed on to children. Others have conditions that may or may not prove serious and need to look to their blood family for clues. Some people simply want to know if their ancestors tended to die early or late, to go bald or keep their hair, to get fat or keep their figures. There is no way they can know without finding their relatives by birth.

So, for whatever reasons, the searchers start off. They don't know what will happen, but they do seem to know, in a general way, what they want—and don't want—out of their quest. They *don't* want to trade their adoptive family in for their birth family. Though this is the adoptive parents' greatest fear, it's hardly ever what the adoptees have in mind. They don't imagine themselves calling their birth mother "mom" and turning to her for mothering; after all, she's a complete stranger. Even when the birth mothers want to mother them, few searchers welcome it. In most people's lives, there's room for only one mother.

All the searchers really insist on is contact. They want to see and talk with the mother who bore them. They want to ask the questions that have always been with them: "Why did you give me up?" and "Who are my relatives?" If it turns out that there's no room for them in their mother's life (or no room for her in theirs), that's all right. All that's important is that they meet.

Searchers don't want to drop into their birth mother's life like a bomb. They are usually careful to consider her feelings. They spend a long time thinking up tactful ways to announce themselves, for instance. ("Hi, this is the daughter you gave up for adoption" is a bit blunt and shocking.) They are aware that their birth mother may have a husband and family who know nothing about the child she gave up, and they are careful not to barge into her life and reveal her secrets. "I was aware of the very real possibility that my mother simply would not want to see me," said one adoptee, "that I might be opening a door in her life long closed and better left that way; in short, that I would be invading her privacy." Another person had a similar sympathetic attitude: "I did not wish, under any circumstances, to intrude upon the life of anyone, yet I could no longer quell my need for a bit of family history. . . . And, not incidentally, I wanted (rather, hoped) to discover that I had not ruined my birth parents' lives by my inconvenient appearance into this world."

Having decided to proceed—carefully, fearfully, but also with tremendous excitement—adoptees steel themselves for the battle against the sealed records. Those who were adopted through an agency can go there and get "non-identifying" information about their birth parents. A person might learn, for example, that his mother was twenty-two when he was born, that her background was German, and that she was working as a secretary at the time. But the adoptee couldn't find out her last name or her current address. The agency will describe his mother; they won't tell who she is or where she is.

Adoptees know the day they were born, and sometimes they know the name of the city in which they were born. But their original birth certificates, which include the names of birth parents, and the adoption papers, which were signed by both sets of parents at the time of the adoption, are in a sealed file. In all but four states, the law forbids the adopted person to see it.

So most adoptees begin the search with only one or two tiny clues. Florence Fisher, for example, who as a child had found her adoption paper at the bottom of a drawer, knew the name she had been given at birth, and she knew that her birth mother *might* have come from Philadelphia. Clues like that aren't much to go on. It's as if a detective had to solve a murder on the basis of a hair and a foot-

print. The adoptee who takes on the search has to become
a detective.

Florence Fisher's story is a good example of what the
typical searcher goes through. Her first step was to call
the man who had been the family doctor when she was a
child. It turned out that he had been the doctor who de-
livered her. He had known both her birth mother and her
adoptive mother and had, in fact, arranged the adoption.
But he refused to tell her anything about her birth mother.
"It's none of your business," he said.

Next she wrote to the Bureau of Vital Statistics in Brooklyn, where she'd grown up. She asked for a copy of her
birth certificate, signing the name she'd seen on the adoption paper, Anna Fisher. (Her adoptive name was Ladden;
later she changed it to her birth father's name.) After two
weeks, she received the certificate, and on it were the
name and address of her mother. The address, of course,
was of the place where her mother had lived when she was
born more than twenty years before.

She went there—it was an old apartment building in
Brooklyn—and knocked on all the doors. No one, however,
remembered anyone of her mother's name.

Then she tried the hospital where she'd been born.
Again, she found herself at a dead end. The people at the
hospital, committed to keeping their records on adopted
children private, refused to tell her anything.

The telephone book was her next hope. Both her mother's
and her father's names—Cohen and Fisher—were common,
but she called all the ones that seemed likely in both
New York and Philadelphia. "I'm looking for a Frederick
Fisher," she would say (or a Florence Cohen). "He lived
in New York around twenty years ago." But once again,
she got nowhere.

She felt stuck. She couldn't think of any new approaches
to try, so she simply repeated the old ones over and over.

For instance, she continued to call the hospital where she'd been born. She called every few weeks for years, hoping to get someone on the line who'd be willing to look up her records. She went back to the old apartment building, hoping to find someone who remembered her mother. She called Cohens and Fishers listed in phone books. She spent hours with directories in the library. For years, no new clues turned up. Her search was at a standstill.

Then one day she made her routine call to the hospital and heard an unfamiliar voice at the other end. Instead of hanging up on her, this woman found the files Florence requested and, not realizing they were confidential, read them to her over the phone. Florence heard her grandparents' names and learned that they had come from Russia. That was all, but it was enough to open some new paths.

At first they led nowhere. She strained her eyes looking at forty-year-old phone books on microfilm in the library, but Morris Cohen was no easier to pin down than Frederick Fisher. It was only after she met a lawyer who was willing to help her and a genealogist at the library who became interested in her search that she began to make progress. She attacked her library research with new energy, discovering that all kinds of records—not just phone books—could be helpful to her. She pored over birth records, marriage licenses, voter registration records, immigration records, census records. Little by little, she added to her store of information: she found the address where her grandparents had lived in 1933, she learned that her parents had been married at the time of her birth, she found the dates of her grandparents' deaths, and finally— after endless conversations with strangers, phone calls to offices, hospitals, churches, funeral homes, hours of checking long lists of names and addresses—she learned her mother's present last name. Fortunately, it was an unusual one. Within a few days, she had found her phone number and spoken to her for the first time. The search had taken her twenty years.

Countless adoptees have gone through more or less the same process. Some are lucky enough to find their birth mothers in a matter of months, weeks, or even days. Others, like Florence Fisher, pursue the search for years. Betty Jean Lifton, who made her own search and has also talked to dozens of adoptees about theirs, has divided the typical search into stages. No two searches are identical, of course. But, when you've heard about enough of them, you can see similar patterns.

There's the beginning phase, which Lifton calls "crossing the threshold." The adoptee makes up her mind and takes the first step. This might mean visiting an adoption agency or calling a hospital. Some people begin by petitioning the court to open the sealed records. The law in most states allows for the opening of the records if the adoptee can prove she has "good cause." Deciding whether the cause is good or not is up to the judge. Sometimes health reasons are judged good cause, as are reasons having to do with property rights. Most often, however, the cause is judged not good enough, and the records remain closed.

These first steps are often made in a rather businesslike spirit. The adoptee mails some letters, asks a few people for information, looks up some data more or less as if she were doing a magazine article about someone else. But then the roadblocks begin to appear. Clerks tell the searcher the files are none of her business; judges decide against her; promising clues lead nowhere. Instead of dampening her enthusiasm, though, all this frustration just turns the spark into a flame. The searcher grows angry and becomes more determined than ever.

One man, at this stage of his search, expressed his feelings this way: "No one, no social worker had the right to decide for me what I should know about me. If I don't like what I find out, that's my problem. I'm an adult in every other way, and I make my own decisions about what risks I take, and I face the consequences, too. You can't understand what it feels like to sit across the desk from a strange social worker who asks you, 'Why do you need to know?' Instead, the question really should be, 'Why wouldn't you need to know?' She was reading my record, my life, and pulling out little tidbits that she decided she would let me taste. I was so angry inside, but I kept my cool, because I wanted whatever information I could get. Who has a better right to that record than I do?"

At this point, the search can become an obsession. Some people let it take over their lives. They postpone decisions about their careers or their families in order to devote all their time and energy to their search. Students who become involved in it usually find that searching and studying don't mix. Many adoptees conduct their search in secret because they don't want their adoptive families to know about it. This can add an air of intrigue and excitement to the whole thing. The search becomes a kind of fascinating game, as hard to put down as a good thriller.

Obsession may hold the searcher in its grip right to the end, or it may give way to a waiting period, a kind of limbo. Suddenly doubts and fears take over again. The searcher has a good deal of information, perhaps even enough to make the contact. But she hesitates, afraid to take that final step. Does she really want to know? Can she face whatever happens next? Sometimes searchers hover in a state of indecision for years.

But eventually, having come this far, most searchers take the final step, which Lifton calls "penetrating the veil." This is the call, or the letter, or the knock on the door that leads finally to the reunion. It means trading in all the years of imaginings for reality.

And the reality can be just about anything, from a dream come true to a nightmare. Usually it's somewhere in between. The searcher finds a nice, ordinary middle-aged woman with a husband and family. She may be glad to see her long-lost child; some mothers have never stopped hoping that the child they gave up would someday find them, and some have actually been searching themselves. Or the mother may be so shocked to be discovered, and so anxious to keep her secret, that she denies everything and insists that the searcher has made a mistake. She may relent later, after she has recovered from the initial shock, and admit who she is, or she may not. Some searchers (but only about one in a hundred) just have to accept the fact that their birth mothers, for whom they have searched so long and hard, have no desire to know them.

Florence Fisher's mother was one of the many who waver between acceptance and denial. When she first met Florence, she denied everything. "You have made a mistake," she said. "I am not the person you're looking for." It was not until a few days later that she called Florence and arranged another meeting. This time she admitted that she was Florence's mother. She said she had been so shocked the first time they'd met that she felt as if a building had caved in on her. She simply hadn't known what to say.

Florence and her birth mother saw each other several times, often enough for Florence to learn what she wanted to know about her heritage and to feel the connection that she'd been missing for so long. Then they went separate ways and did not meet again. This seems to happen fairly often with these reunions, for one reason or another. Betty Jean Lifton, in *Lost and Found,* describes several such experiences. One adoptee, for instance, found her mother in a mental hospital, unable to speak and almost totally unresponsive to other people. They met only once. Another person found a mother she simply didn't like, a woman who seemed to her shallow and insensitive. Their relationship, also, was brief.

But some birth mothers invite their newfound children

back into the family, almost as if they had always been there. For the adoptee who's been an only child, or whose adoptive parents have died, or who has never really felt like part of a family, this can be wonderful. For others, it can be awkward. The searcher may not want to become part of the birth mother's family. He may not have time for them; he may not feel comfortable with them. On the one hand, he doesn't want to reject the person he's looked for so long. On the other hand, he doesn't want to accept what she wants to offer.

An adopted child's reunion with his birth mother is a peculiar kind of occurrence, one that's outside the bounds of ordinary social interactions. Once the actual meeting has been accomplished, the adoptee and the birth mother sometimes don't quite know what to do next. What are they to each other, anyhow? They're not exactly family, because they don't have the years of association that bind family members together. They're not necessarily friends; they're of different generations and may have totally different ways of life. Their connection is very basic, and yet it may not be strong enough to hold them together for more than one encounter.

Because of this, adoptees may suddenly find themselves in situations they don't know how to handle. "[My birth mother] doesn't understand she is making demands I can't meet," said one adoptee, "like calling her 'mother.'"

"What is our responsibility to our mothers?" asks another adoptee, whose birth mother is ill. "For example, do we owe them financial assistance?"

Many adoptees find that the tremendous emotional high of the reunion gives way to confusion or depression later on. To have a myth turned into a reality is a psychological shock, even if the actual reunion is a good one. A huge change has taken place in the adoptee's life, and his mind and emotions have to make major readjustments. Those readjustments can sometimes throw a person out of whack for a while. Some adoptees have terrible nightmares. Some become unreasonably anxious and afraid. Some even become physically ill.

In addition to their own reactions, searchers have to cope with the reactions of their adoptive families, who are likely to be profoundly uneasy about what their son or daughter is doing. Their worst fear is that their child is going to say, "Well, I've found my real mother now; I don't need you anymore." At best, they imagine that whatever affection their child shares with his birth parents will somehow detract from his affections for them.

Knowing this, adoptees may feel guilty about their search, fearful that it will damage their adoptive family relationships, and they may be both angry with and protective of their adoptive parents. They may never tell their mother and father about their search at all, either because they think their parents cannot handle it or because they dread their parents' anger and hurt feelings. Some adoptees who do tell their parents meet with just the sort of reaction they've been afraid of. "How could you be so ungrateful?" their parents say. "Haven't we been good parents to you? How could you care so little for our feelings?" Or they may say nothing at all, and from then on they may act as though the subject had never been mentioned. It's the same kind of silence and denial that they've practiced on the subject of adoption all along.

But a surprising number of parents can accept their children's search and even take pleasure in it. In fact, three researchers who collected reunion stories from a great many adoptees were struck by how often the adoptees' search made their relationships with their adoptive family better. The secrets were all out at last, and everyone could relax. The adopted child had found the birth parents but had not vanished from the adoptive family. And the adoptee had gained valuable new understanding of the roles of both sets of parents. In the book they wrote about their findings, *The Adoption Triangle*, by Arthur D. Sorosky, Annette Baran, and Reuben Pannor, the researchers state without hesitation that "a primary benefit of the reunion experience is the strengthening of the adoptive family relationship."

In one story after another, adoptees describe this experience, often with amazement:

"Perhaps the most surprising change of all has been my growing awareness that I am, for better or worse, the child of my adoptive parents. . . . I see them in me, in a way I never could when I spent so much time wondering."

"My adoptive parents began to share their feelings with me; their fear of rejection, feelings of inadequacy at not being able to give birth to their own children. Because everyone was able to give of themselves through the expression of their feelings, I have a better understanding of myself."

"My parents seemed truly happy that I had met my birth mother, had found out so much about my early life, and that I had a half-sister and family living so close. Their understanding of the situation has made my estimation of them rise a great deal."

And what about the searchers themselves? After the years of wondering, the complicated detective work, the shock of reunion, how do they feel about what they've done?

Judging by their accounts, they feel just fine. Betty Jean Lifton says, "I don't know of any adoptee who is sorry she has searched—no matter whom she finds." That's saying a lot, since many searchers find family histories that are extremely disturbing. An adoptee may discover, for example, that his birth mother was raped, and that his birth was the result of that crime. Sometimes an adoptee will find out that his birth parents' relationship was incestuous. One man, for instance, learned that his mother had become pregnant by her father and that therefore his father and his grandfather were the same person. There's the chance, too, that the birth parents were neglectful or abusive, like the teenage mother who kept her child in a dresser drawer, used rags for diapers, and paid so little attention to her that the child became weak and listless and at the age of six months neither laughed, smiled, nor cried.

Revelations like these are hard to take. And yet even people whose early histories turn out to be ugly or deprived usually say they're glad to know. A woman named Sylvia, for example, learned that her father had been severly disturbed and had killed both her mother and himself when she was a year old. To have this knowledge instead of the "evil shadows she had felt surrounded by" was actually a relief. The known, however terrible, is often easier to live with than the unknown.

Most adoptees who search for their origins do not unearth such traumatic events. They may find a mother they don't like—one who drinks too much, for instance, or one who seems coarse and ignorant and who makes them realize that being adopted has given them a better life than they would otherwise have had. They may find a mother with whom they have nothing in common, either in looks or in character. But the particular person they find doesn't seem to be the most important thing. What counts is laying the questions to rest and knowing the truth.

"I am very happy," said one woman who had found her birth mother. "I feel whole, as if I have been reunited with myself."

"I know now that I acquired some things from my adoptive family and inherited others from my birth family," another searcher said. "Knowing this affects my personality, my makeup, my sense of who I am."

"It was a long, hard struggle, but I've never regretted it," said a woman who, although she learned that her birth mother was dead, was reunited with her father. "I know my true heritage. Now I feel complete."

The long, hard struggle and the sense of completeness at the end of it are well known to most adoptees who succeed in their searches. Although they feel that searching for their birth parents was an extremely important experience, they may also be filled with resentment for having had to search at all. If the adoption records had been open to them, they could have spared themselves long years of tedious tracking and emotional, and often financial, wear and tear. Adoptees who feel this way have formed organizations to work for change in adoption laws and to help adoptees who want to look for their origins. (Some of these groups are listed in the section Sources of Help at the end of this book.) At the same time, adoptive parents and birth parents are telling their own stories and expressing their own opinions, which are sometimes vigorously opposed to those of the searching adoptees. The whole issue, charged with strong emotions on both sides, has become public and demands action.

CHAPTER *7*

The
Struggle
for
Change

Imagine a family we'll call the Morrises—Lou and Linda
Morris and their adopted daughter Janet, who is eighteen.
Janet's birth mother is a woman named Barbara Harper,
whom Janet and her parents do not know.

An article appears in the newspaper one evening. The
headline says, "Adoption Records: Should They Be Un-
sealed?" and the story gives various experts' opinions on
the subject and describes some proposed changes in the
adoption laws. Janet reads the article when she gets home
from school. Later in the evening, her parents read it. And
the same night, in another city, Barbara Harper reads it,
too.

Suppose we ask these people for their reactions to what
they've read. They might respond like this:

JANET MORRIS: I'm eighteen now; by law, I'm an
adult. I ought to be allowed to see the records. I
want to know about my heritage. After all, it's a
part of me; I have the right to see it.

LOU AND LINDA MORRIS: When we adopted Janet, we
became her only real parents. We were told that
the adoption records would always be sealed. If
they are opened, will the birth mother come here
and make a claim on Janet? Would Janet leave us

99

for her? We don't want this to happen. We have the right to keep our family intact.

BARBARA HARPER: I often think about the baby I gave up for adoption. I wonder if she is happy and well, and I wonder what kind of person she is. I know I gave her up eighteen years ago. At the time, I didn't see any other choice. But that doesn't mean I don't care what happened to her. I think I have the right to know.

Or perhaps Barbara Harper might answer this way:

When I signed the adoption papers, I ended all my parental responsibilities. That was a painful time in my life; I want to forget it. Now I have a husband and children who don't know about my past. I want to keep it that way. I think I have a right to my privacy.

Of all these rights, whose comes first? It's important to decide, because granting what some people see as their right will mean infringing on what other people see as theirs. As long as no one challenged the secrecy of the records, the problem didn't arise. But now people—mainly adoptees who want to learn the facts about themselves—are challenging it, and the traditional adoption procedure is being pushed little by little toward change.

The center of the controversy is the sealed file. In that file is the adoptee's original birth certificate with the names of the original mother and father. A child who is adopted is issued a new birth certificate with the name of the adoptive parents. The old certificate is supposed to remain permanently secret. (This is the case in all except five states: Alabama, Kansas, South Dakota, New Jersey, and Minnesota.)

This secrecy became a standard part of adoption policy

in the 1930s. Originally, the purpose of it was to protect adopted children, who were usually born out of wedlock, from the stigma of illegitimacy. No one wanted these children to go through life with "illegitimate" stamped on their birth certificates; in those days, that label was considered shameful, a social handicap. And not only the child but also the adoptive family and the birth mother could be embarrassed by it. There was always the possibility that someone might find out this damaging information and use it against them. If the birth and adoption records were sealed, however, everyone involved was protected.

Today, most people don't consider an illegitimate child any less worthy than a legitimate one. After all, how the child came into the world is not the child's fault. Young women are far less embarrassed than they used to be about having babies out of wedlock and also about keeping those babies and raising them. So everyone has less reason to fear that the word "illegitimate" will make a black mark on their lives.

But if the original reason for sealing the adoption records has more or less faded away, other reasons have evolved that are just as powerful, if not more so. The general opinion has come to be that sealing the records keeps the adoptive family intact. If the birth mother doesn't know the names of the adoptive parents, she can't intrude on them, looking for her child. If the child doesn't know the name of her birth mother, she can't intrude on her, looking for her heritage. Everyone is protected from everyone else, and no one has to worry about the sudden knock on the door that disrupts the course of life.

The guarantee of privacy for all parties has become adoption agency policy. Without it, adoption workers say, birth mothers wouldn't be willing to surrender their babies. They'd be too afraid that someday those grown up babies would come looking for them, exposing the secrets of their past to the world.

The feelings expressed by some birth mothers support this fear. "I had an illegitimate child when I was nineteen," one woman said. "No one knew about it except my parents. Three years later I got married. My husband has no idea of my past nor will he be told. I now have a prestigious job, a child, and a lovely home. I am now thirty years of age. I'm afraid that if the child ever came to my front door it would be the end of my marriage. My husband would probably get custody of our child.

"I have closed all doors behind me for my protection and peace of mind. I do not want them opened by a curious child."

Another birth mother who feels this way imagines what might happen if the files were not kept secret: "It is possible that if birth records do become routinely available to adoptees that a birth mother who wants to keep her identity a secret may have to go to greater lengths to do so. Babies have been known to be found on doorsteps in the past. Let's hope that this does not become the alternative."

If all birth mothers felt this way, the argument for keeping the records sealed would be strong. No one wants to frighten birth mothers away from adoption agencies and compel them instead to leave their babies in baskets with notes pinned to their blankets. But there's also evidence that opening the birth records wouldn't necessarily cause this to happen.

Although some women might be less likely to place their babies for adoption if they knew the child they'd given up could some day find them, many others might actually be more likely to. On paper, adoption as it is today sounds like an easy thing for the birth mother: have the baby, sign the papers, and walk away a free woman, ready to put the whole experience behind you. In reality, it's rarely that simple. Many women find that their feelings about having a baby are unexpectedly strong. They have a hard time resigning themselves to the fact that they'll never know what happens to their child. They find, contrary to what the agency has told them, that they don't forget the whole experience at all. Sometimes they feel that it would be easier to give the child up if they weren't going to lose track of it completely and forever.

A number of birth mothers described feelings like these to the research team led by Arthur Sorosky. In the letters they wrote, many of the same phrases appear again and again:

"I want to explain to him why he was given up for adoption."

"I want her to know that she was not rejected."

"I have never forgotten the daughter I gave up for adoption."

"I think about her every day and will always love her."

"I think about him constantly."

"I would like to tell him about me and why I gave him up for adoption."

"I would give anything in the world to know more about him."

These women have not put the experience of having a child behind them. They feel oppressed, not protected, by the privacy the adoption agency guarantees.

Many birth mothers, like many adoptees, believe that this secrecy is not a protection of their rights but an infringement on them, and they are pressing for a change in the sealed-record policy. There's even an organization called Concerned United Birthparents (CUB), composed of people who have surrendered children for adoption, whose purpose is to change adoption policies so that an adopted child may see the records when he or she becomes an adult.

So some adoptees and some birth mothers favor opening the records. Some adoptive parents favor it, too, though probably not nearly as large a percentage. In general, adoptive parents are more likely to think that closed records serve their interests best. One parent, for example, protests: "We were assured that the original birth certificate would be sealed for all time. Now, however, in another court somewhere, a judge may well hand out a ruling that will upset all this by changing a facet of the adoption process that has long been regarded as essential. At stake is not only the traditional relationship between adoption agencies and adopting couples but the relationship between many children and their adoptive parents." Unsealing the records is seen as a real danger, as though the discovery of those other parents would automatically be damaging to the adoptive family.

If you invited a group of adoptees, birth parents, and adoptive parents to discuss the sealed records issue, you'd probably hear a debate with not just three sides but six or more. Some people in each category would vote "closed," and some would vote "open." The votes might line up something like this:

> Adoptee 1: Open the records. I need to know my heritage.
>
> Adoptee 2: Keep the records closed. I have no interest in the woman who gave me up.
>
> Birth Mother 1: Open the records. I want to know what became of my child.
>
> Birth Mother 2: Keep the records closed. I don't want my life disrupted.
>
> Adoptive Parent 1: Open the records. My child has a right to know where he comes from.
>
> Adoptive Parent 2: Keep the records closed. I don't want my family destroyed.

If you polled all the people in the country who might have an opinion on the subject—including psychologists and social workers—you might find that the votes for "closed" and "open" were equal. Or you might find that one side far outweighed the other or that many votes couldn't be counted as either for "closed" or for "open" but had to be considered somewhere in between. No one, of course, has taken such a poll, so no one knows what the results would be.

Right now, however, the "closed" side has the power, simply because the records are already closed. It's usually easier to keep something the way it is than to change it. Those who advocate change have to make a very convincing case in order to alter what is already established. The question is, have the adoption reformers made a good case for opening the sealed records?

Let's look at some of the arguments. Probably the most vocal are the adoptees, whom we heard from in Chapter 6. Their plea for change is based on their need to know where they came from, as other people do. Clearly, they are not saying they want to go back where they came from, abandoning their adoptive families. But they believe they have the right to know. Certain psychologists have affirmed the importance of this need to connect with the blood family. And the number of adoptee search groups that have been founded all over the country attests to the strength of the need. Betty Jean Lifton lists thirty-six such groups in her book *Lost and Found*, and more are being started all the time.

The birth parents who have taken a stand in favor of open records are fewer than the adoptees. Guilt and shame over being unwed mothers and fear of what other people will think has kept most of them from making their opinions public. But in recent years, as people have begun to talk more openly about adoption, birth mothers are speaking up. One woman, Lorraine Dusky, has written a book called *Birthmark*, in which she describes her own experience.

Lorraine Dusky was twenty-two and just beginning a career in journalism when she realized she was pregnant.

The child's father was married and had children of his own. He promised he would divorce his wife and marry Lorraine, but in the end he changed his mind, and she had the baby, keeping it a secret from nearly everyone she knew. Because she was alone and because she wanted very much to go on with her career, she decided that adoption was her only choice. She never saw the daughter she had borne, but she never forgot about her, either. The pain of the experience and the hope of someday finding out what happened to her child have been with her ever since. She writes:

I am always looking for my daughter. Girl, weighing four pounds four ounces at birth, April 5, 1966, in upstate New York. Baptized: Mary. Her birth is the single most important event of my life; since that day, her existence has shaped who I am. I live in the hope that someday I might be able to telephone her on her birthday and send her flowers or a ticket to someplace she would like to go. I would like to ask her how things turned out and if her parents are nice to her and if they love her.

I know, I know, I gave her away, I can hear you thinking; I knew what I was doing and so why am I making a fuss now?

A signature cannot abrogate my feelings.

As things stand now, the yearning and searching will go on until I find her.

It is likely that many birth mothers feel this way, at least to some degree, even though they may hesitate to say so. Those who have spoken or written about their feelings make it clear that they didn't just toss their babies away without a thought and forget them. They felt great pain at the separation, real concern for the child's future, and often a lasting guilt and anxiety that could not be alleviated except by finding out what happened to the child. They want the records opened, not so much to enable them to find their lost children but to enable the children to find them.

Another argument for opening the records has to do with the adoptive parents. Parents are likely to think that keeping the records closed is best for their families. Some of the people who have studied adoptive families, however, believe that just the opposite is true—that "the aura of secrecy has been more of a burden than a protection to adoptive parents." Keeping the secret means keeping up the pretense that the birth parents don't exist, even though everyone knows this isn't true. It means not talking about them, even though both child and parents probably think about them frequently. It means that what's happening on the surface doesn't match what's happening underneath, a state of affairs that's more likely to push people away from each other than draw them together.

Whether or not all these feelings and opinions add up to a good case for opening the records is something that, eventually, the lawmakers will have to decide. And if they decide that changing adoption policies is a good idea, they won't just declare, "All adoption records are now open, and anyone who wants to can look at them." It won't be nearly that simple.

For one thing, most people agree that records should be accessible only to adoptees who have reached a certain age—eighteen, for instance, or twenty-one. If information is available sooner, it might just cause confusion and upset. Someone of fourteen, for example, might have the curiosity to seek out his birth parents but not the maturity to deal with the resulting complicated situation. There are people who disagree here, however. Betty Jean Lifton thinks adopted children ought to know all the facts about themselves by the time they're thirteen. She does not think that they should necessarily meet their birth parents at that time, but if they have a better idea of who they are and where they come from, Lifton believes, they might avoid a lot of the confusion and turmoil that adopted teenagers often suffer through.

In some cases, one person wants a reunion and the other doesn't. Suppose adoptee Jane wants to meet her birth mother Phyllis, but Phyllis has no desire to meet Jane. What then? If the records were opened, Jane could seek out Phyllis whether Phyllis wanted to be found or not. According to some opinions, this is an infringement of Phyllis's right to privacy. According to others, however, Phyllis does not have the right to privacy from the child she gave birth to. They say that Jane's right to know her origins comes first.

One way around this dilemma was first suggested by Jean Paton, an adoption activist who founded an organization called Orphan Voyage. Her idea is a reunion file, a place where information about the adoptee and about the birth parents could be written down and kept current over the years. The birth mother would be able to look at the file from time to time as her child was growing up. What she read would be nonidentifying information. She might learn, for example, that her child was doing well in school or showed talent in art, but not where he lived or what the adoptive parents' name was. When the child becomes a legal adult, then either he or the birth mother could express a desire to meet the other. The reunion would take place only if both parties wanted it.

The Child Welfare League of America, aware of the increasing pressure for change in adoption laws, has recommended that adoption agencies tell birth parents and adoptive parents that they can no longer guarantee confidentiality. Sooner or later, the laws might be changed, and that guarantee could no longer be upheld. Some agencies have already changed their policies and are giving searching adoptees their whole files instead of just the nonidentifying information. These files are separate from the court records. Other agencies have offered to act as mediators in reunions. If an adopted person comes back to the agency wanting information about his birth mother, agency staff members will get in touch with her and, if she agrees, arrange the meeting.

Many adoptees, however, don't want agencies to get into the reunion business. A meeting with your birth mother is a very private thing, in their opinion, and a third party has no place in it. They would rather make contacts and arrange reunions themselves. They also resent the counseling that agencies often require them to have. All they want is that the records be opened; the rest they insist they can take care of themselves.

If the records are to be opened, the law must be changed, and adoption activists are working on several fronts to make that happen. Individuals and organizations have filed lawsuits that challenge the sealed records. The Adoptees' Liberty Movement Association (ALMA), for example, has filed a suit saying that sealing adoption records is unconstitutional, that it deprives adopted children of the right to be whole people. That suit is now before the U.S. Supreme Court.

Many adoptees have taken their cases to court, hoping for decisions that will allow them to gain access to their records and that will also set precedents to benefit other adoptees. One law they've attacked is the one that says adoptees may see their birth records only if they can prove in court that they have "good cause." Usually, good cause has to be something fairly urgent—a pressing question of health, or a decision about property rights. But a lawyer named Gertrud Mainzer won a case in which she argued that every adult adoptee has good cause and should be entitled to see the records because the information in them is important for social adjustment. This decision may pave the way for other adoptees who petition the court for their records.

In some states, legislators have proposed bills that would change the adoption laws. A bill proposed in California in 1980, for example, would have allowed adoptees over twenty-one to see their records. The bill failed to pass, however, and this might also be the fate of similar bills that have been proposed in New York, Oklahoma, and Utah. But others like them are sure to be offered in the future. Legal opinion seems to be changing, slowly but surely, to favor the right of the adoptee to see the records.

Imagine that the disagreement over the sealed records was suddenly all smoothed out and that laws all over the country were changed to allow adoptees of eighteen or over to see their files. Suppose this change was to take effect next week. On Monday morning, would hundreds of adopted people be standing in line at agencies to find out about their birth parents?

It's not very likely. Although we don't know for sure what would happen, we do have a way of guessing. This is to look at the results in Britain of the Children's Act of 1975, which opened birth records to adopted people over the age of eighteen. The law was enacted in spite of vehement protests against it, from both adoptive parents and birth parents and also from adoption agency employees, who feared the law would upset family relationships and weaken the traditional adoption process. Five years later, however, it's becoming apparent that the predicted disasters are not occurring.

Very few of the adopted people who could have applied for information about themselves actually did so—in fact, only one or two percent. And not all of those who did look at their records went on to seek out their birth parents. The ones who did search did so responsibly and sensitively, with no intent to disrupt anyone's life.

In a report to the British Parliament, the Department of Health and Social Services wrote that people's fears about the results of the Children's Act were unfounded. Adoptive families were not being shattered; birth mothers' lives were not being ruined by insensitive adoptees. Instead, more and more people—both adoptees and birth mothers—were writing and speaking about adoption and how it has affected them. Instead of being divisive, the Children's Act may actually be contributing to a better understanding of adoption and a drawing together of the people involved in it.

Opening the records is, all by itself, enough to satisfy adoptees who want to know their origins. But there are also many birth mothers who want the right to meet the children they gave up. A law like the Children's Act in England does not grant birth mothers this right. The adoption records remain closed to them permanently. The same would probably be true if adoption laws were changed in the United States. This confronts the birth mother thinking about placing her baby for adoption with a black and white choice: she must either give the child up and resign herself to never knowing what becomes of it and never seeing it again, or she must keep it and raise it herself. The only other hope, and it's a slim one, is that in twenty years or so, her grown-up child will find her and tell her what his life has been like.

With adoption practices as they now are, there's no way around this dilemma. But a new kind of adoption has been suggested recently that might offer another choice. It is called open adoption, and its advocates say it has benefits for the birth mother, the child, and the adoptive parents as well.

In an open adoption, the birth mother knows the adoptive family and keeps some contact with her child. Suppose, for example, that an open adoption had been arranged for Janet Morris, whose family we talked about at the beginning of this chapter. It might have worked something like this:

Barbara Harper, Janet's birth mother, explains her situation to a social worker. She realizes that she can't take care of Janet very well. She can't get a job that will bring in enough money, and, at eighteen, she has discovered that being a mother makes demands on her time, her energy, and her feelings that she just can't meet. But she can't bear the idea of being separated from her baby forever, either. "I would feel so guilty," she says "just giving her away, not knowing where she was going, never being able to see her again. It would be so painful, like having a part of my body cut off."

The social worker knows of a couple, the Morrises, who might be willing to consider an open adoption. Barbara and the Morrises meet to talk about it. Barbara likes them; she sees that they can give Janet the kind of care she can't. The three of them agree to the adoption.

Barbara legally transfers all the responsibility for raising Janet to the Morrises. She will not have the right to decide how Janet is brought up, even if she disagrees with the Morrises' decisions, but she keeps the right to visit her daughter occasionally. Together, she and the Morrises work out when those visits will be, how long they'll last, and how often they will take place. As Janet grows older, Barbara's role in her life will be explained to her. She will understand that her heritage is double—both adoptive and biological—and she will not be preoccupied by the questions that most adopted children turn over and over in their heads: Who is my birth mother? Why did she give me up?

Barbara won't have to face either the permanent loss of her child or the great responsibility of caring for her. And the Morrises will benefit from the openness of the whole situation: they'll have no secrets to keep from Janet and no need to dread her questions. The "other mother," being a person and not a mystery, won't have the power to grow unnaturally large in anyone's imagination. The scene described at the beginning of this chapter, in which they all disagree about Janet's right to see her birth records, will never take place.

It's not hard, of course, to foresee problems with an open adoption. What if the birth mother objects to the way the adoptive parents are raising her child and tries to interfere? What if she later regrets her decision to give up her rights and begins to compete with the adoptive parents for the child's affection? Would the child in an open adoption become confused about who the "real" mother is? Would couples be less willing to adopt if they had to deal with the birth mother?

At this point, no one is suggesting that traditional adoptions be totally replaced by open ones. For many people, an open adoption wouldn't be acceptable at all. Still, in some way or other, it looks as though traditional adoption is headed for change.

The target of the change is the secret—that folder of papers in the agency file cabinet labeled "Confidential" and closed forever to those it concerns most. Some people say the success of adoption depends on secrecy. Others say that secrecy, in the long run, can only be destructive. Who's right?

There's no easy answer. Any problem involving human emotions is bound to be complicated and delicate, not cut and dried like a mathematical equation. In the end, a decision about opening the sealed birth records, or making any other change in the workings of adoption, will come not because somebody at last discovers the truth of the matter, but because those who make the decision have listened carefully to many different points of view. They will have to listen to pregnant teenagers trying to decide on the best course, to adoptive parents fearful of losing their child, to adoptees who can't rest until they know where they came from. They will have to read all kinds of accounts of feelings and experiences and, with an open mind, try to see what they all add up to, because if adoption is going to change, it is from these life stories that the new direction will come.

Epilogue: Scenes from Two Lives

When Priscilla decided to investigate her birth heritage, she found that the sealed records blocked her way like a wall. She knew the adoption agency had the information she wanted—the names of her birth parents, the tribes they belonged to, where they had lived twenty-two years ago —but legally the agency could not give it to her. With the help of an organization called Operation Identity, Priscilla decided to take her case to court.

All adoptees have to prove that they have good cause for wanting their records opened, and since a good cause usually has to be an especially urgent one, it can be hard to prove. But Priscilla thought she had a chance at it. She'd discovered that she had a disease of the red blood cells, one that was uncommon in the United States and that doctors were unsure how to treat. If she knew her biological background, she would argue, she might learn something about this disease—where it came from, how to deal with it, whether there was danger of passing it on to her children. These ought to be compelling enough reasons to warrant the opening of her file.

While the case was pending, she did some research of her own. She read avidly about Ethiopia and its tribes and customs. She tracked down some Ethiopians who were in the United States and questioned them, hoping what they

115

said might fill in some of the empty spots in her skeleton of a story. And little by little, she picked up clues.

She learned, for example, that her mother probably belonged to one of five ruling-class Ethiopian families, since her mother's father had held a high position that only a person from one of those families could have filled. She learned about the rigid social system that governed the upper classes at the time of her birth, involving arranged marriages, strict codes of moral behavior, and stern punishments for those who broke them. She learned about the history of Ethiopia (the fact that Ethiopians had never been brought to this country as slaves was especially interesting) and about the current turmoil there—the civil war that has been raging since the early 1960s. She even began to learn Amharic, the official language of Ethiopia. Although her search was slow and frustrating, it was turning out to be tremendously educational.

Gary's search for his birth mother lasted only a day and a half. He already knew her last name, and he found her first name by going through voting records in the city where he knew he'd been born. A marriage license giving the names of some of her relatives helped him to pinpoint an address where his mother and her husband had lived several years before. He went there—it was an apartment building—and started knocking on doors.

"I'm a friend of someone who used to live here," he told the people who answered, giving the name of his birth mother's husband. "Did you happen to know him or his wife?" It didn't take long to find a neighbor who had. She told Gary that the husband had died and that his wife had moved to another state. "I can give you her current address and phone number, if you like," she added.

"Thank you," stammered Gary. "That would be great." His search was over already. He decided he would call his birth mother that very afternoon.

Priscilla doubts that she will ever meet, or see, her birth parents. To appear suddenly in her birth mother's life would be, in her case, far more than inconsiderate. It might actually put her mother's life in danger. Priscilla has no desire to shatter a life in order to satisfy her curiosity.

In fact, Priscilla's quest into her origins doesn't have the urgency of many adoptees'. "I wish my mother had told me that I was adopted," she says, "only because it would have saved her a lot of agony. The secret tormented her for so long. But it was her decision to make. She didn't want me to know, for her own personal reasons, and so I don't think, had I found out, that I'd ever have done any research—at least not during her lifetime."

Still, her birth heritage continues to fascinate her. She has a degree in journalism and experience in filmmaking, and what she'd most like to do is go to Ethiopia and film the place where her own story began. "I want to find out before I go who my people are," she says. "I'd like to be able to say, 'This is my father's ranch, this is the road he must have walked on, this is the school my mother went to.' I'd never really show my mother, of course—unless—unless I get there and a fantastic thing happens, and it's all right to talk to her after all."

In the meantime, Priscilla waits for the court's decision on opening her records, and, for her own satisfaction, finds out everything she can about the country of her ancestors.

"Hello?" said a woman's voice on the other end of the line.

"Is this Maria LoPresti?" Gary asked.

"Yes, it is," the voice replied.

Gary swallowed hard. He had found the right person. But suddenly his nerve was failing him. "We have a bad connection," he said, and he hung up the phone. He needed time to think about this.

A few days later he called again, this time having

planned out what he would say. At first, the woman said she didn't know what he was talking about. But as soon as Gary assured her that he wouldn't reveal anything she wished to keep private, her defenses crumbled. She said she was indeed his mother, and they talked for more than an hour. "I always dreaded that you might try to find me," she said at last. "But now that you have, I'm glad."

About a year later, Gary met his biological family. In addition to his mother, he had a half-sister, three uncles, cousins, and a niece, and they welcomed him warmly. It was exciting to meet people who were related to him by blood and to discover that some of them looked like him. And it was good to find that he liked these people and could have a good time with them.

Gary's search had many rewards. For one thing, he has the satisfaction of knowing he's relieved his birth mother's mind of a burden of guilt that she had carried since he was born. She can see now that he's been happy and well loved; it's clear to her that she did the right thing. Also, Gary has been able to talk about his search and reunion with his adoptive father; because his father understood his need to search, Gary hasn't had to keep it secret for fear of hurting him. And most important, Gary has achieved some peace of mind for himself. He has answered the questions that have been part of his life since its beginning.

All except one. Who was his father? For Gary's birth mother, he was a very brief affair; she doesn't even remember his first name, and she never told him she was pregnant. For Gary, he is an intriguing mystery—one that he hopes someday to solve.

Sources
of
Help

Counseling for Pregnancy and Adoption

Probably the easiest way to find a counseling service is to look in your telephone book under Family Service Association. This organization has branches all over the country. If you don't find a listing, you can write to the following address and ask if there is an agency close to you:

Family Service Association of America
44 East 23rd Street
New York, New York 10010

You might also check in your phone book under the following headings:

Health and Welfare Council
Mental Health Clinic
County or City Department of Health
Council for Community Services
Counseling Clinic
Information and Referral Service

Locating a Maternity Home

The Salvation Army and the Florence Crittenton Association run homes for unmarried pregnant women in many states. Local religious organizations, especially Catholic ones, may also sponsor such homes.

In general, maternity homes offer food, shelter, and medi-

119

cal care. They may also offer counseling, classes in child care, and adoption services.

Adoptee Organizations

These groups offer information to adoptees interested in searching for their birth parents.

Adoptees Liberty Movement Associates
P.O. Box 154
Washington Bridge Station
New York, New York 10033

Adoptees Registry
66 Court Street
Brooklyn, New York 11201

Adoption Research Project
P.O. Box 49809
Los Angeles, California 90049

Orphan Voyage
c/o Jean Paton
Cedaredge, Colorado 81413

Bibliography

Nonfiction

Baker, Nancy C. *Babyselling: The Scandal of Black Market Adoptions.* New York: Vanguard, 1978.

This is an investigation of the illegal market in babies that has been brought about by the baby shortage. The author describes how black market practices can affect the child, the adoptive parents, and the birth mother, and she makes a plea for legal action to end the traffic in babies.

Blank, Joseph P. *19 Steps up the Mountain, The Story of the DeBolt Family.* Philadelphia: Lippincott, 1976.

This book introduces all the members of the DeBolt family, which includes adopted children of several races and with many kinds of handicaps. It's a lively description, complete with pictures, of a remarkable household.

Dusky, Lorraine. *Birthmark.* New York: Evans, 1979.

Lorraine Dusky, who gave up a child for adoption, describes the pain of her experience and the undiminished longing she still feels—and believes that many birth mothers feel—to find and meet the child she could not keep.

Fisher, Florence. *The Search for Anna Fisher.* New York: Fawcett, 1973.

Florence Fisher was one of the first adoptees to write the story of her search for her birth mother. This account stirred up a great deal of interest in the plight of adopted people who need to know their origins.

Lifton, Betty Jean. *Lost and Found: The Adoption Experience.* New York: Dial Press, 1979.

A fascinating study of adopted people in search of their identities. Lifton explores the subject from many angles and in-

121

cludes personal stories of adoptees, birth parents, and adoptive parents.

Lifton, Betty Jean. *Twice Born: Memoirs of an Adopted Daughter.* New York: McGraw-Hill, 1975.
This is Lifton's story of her own experiences as an adopted child and as an adult who searched for her birth mother.

Margolies, Marjorie, and Gruber, Ruth. *They Came to Stay.* New York: Coward, McCann & Geoghegan, 1976.
Marjorie Margolies, a single woman, adopted two children—one Korean and one Vietnamese-American. Her struggle to get these children to the United States and to help them adjust to a new way of life was both difficult and rewarding.

McKuen, Rod. *Finding My Father: One Man's Search for Identity.* Hollywood, Calif.: Cheval, 1976.
McKuen, the popular poet, was not an adopted child, but he was born out of wedlock and grew up without ever knowing his father. This is the story of his search.

Sorosky, Arthur D.; Baran, Annette; and Pannor, Reuben. *The Adoption Triangle.* New York: Doubleday-Anchor, 1978.
This is a study, complete with many case histories, of the effects of sealed records on adopted people, birth parents, and adoptive parents—the three sides of what the authors call "the adoption triangle."

Fiction

Arthur, Ruth M. *Requiem for a Princess.* New York: Atheneum, 1967.
An English girl discovers by accident that she is adopted. A strange experience involving a Spanish girl orphaned in England over three hundred years ago helps her come to terms with her feelings.

Lowry, Lois. *Find a Stranger, Say Goodbye.* Boston: Houghton Mifflin, 1978.
Natalie has always known she was adopted. When she graduates from high school, she decides to find out the circumstances of her birth and to find her mother. With the help of

her family, she starts out on a quest that leads her in unexpected directions.

Neufeld, John. *Edgar Allan.* New York: S. G. Phillips, 1968.
A white couple adopt a young black boy. The problems that follow tear their family and the community apart and force them to realize how complex and difficult interracial adoption is.

Talbot, Charlene Joy. *An Orphan for Nebraska.* New York: Atheneum, 1979.
Kevin, an orphan, lives on the streets of New York City in the 1870s. When he hears that the Children's Aid Society is sending homeless children to Nebraska to live with farm families, he volunteers to go. The story of his experience is based on fact.

Terris, Susan. *Whirling Rainbows.* New York: Doubleday, 1974.
Leah Friedman has spent all her thirteen years with her Jewish adoptive parents, but by birth she is part Polish and part Chippewa Indian. The summer she goes to Camp Winnebago in Wisconsin, she decides to search for her roots.

Index

About The Author

Jeanne DuPrau has been a junior and senior high school teacher, specializing in reading and English. She is now an editor of text materials and a freelance writer. Ms. DuPrau, who was educated at Scripps College and the University of California, lives in northern California.